INDUCED DEVELOPMENT TO GOOD GOVERNANCE

Paradigm Shift in the Concept of Development Administration in the New Millennium

INDUCED DEVELOPMENT TO GOOD GOVERNANCE

Paradigm Shift in the Concept of Development Administration in the New Millennium

R.B. JAIN

and

ANUJ JAIN

DEEP & DEEP PUBLICATIONS PVT. LTD.

F-159, Rajouri Garden, New Delhi - 110 027

INDUCED DEVELOPMENT TO GOOD GOVERNANCE
Paradigm Shift in the Concept of Development Administration in the New Millennium

ISBN 978-81-8450-367-8

Printed in India at MAYUR ENTERPRISES
WZ Plot No. 3, Gujjar Market, Tihar Village, New Delhi - 110 018

Published by DEEP & DEEP PUBLICATIONS PVT. LTD.,
F-159, Rajouri Garden, New Delhi - 110 027 • Phone : 25435369, 25440916
E-mail : ddpubs@gmail.com • ddpbooks@yahoo.co.in
Showroom :
2/13, Ansari Road, Daryaganj, New Delhi - 110 002 • Telefax : 23245122

Dedicated To

HON. SHRI T.N. CHATURVEDIJI
and PROFESSOR O.P. DWIVEDI
Who have been Great Inspirers and Stimulants
in all our Academic Pursuits

Contents

Preface

The concept of "Development Administration" is a post World War II evolution within the discipline of public administration. At the end of World War II, the age of imperialism had come to an end, and the rapid process of de-colonization had begun. By early 1960s, many of the countries in Africa, Latin America, Asia and Middle East had gained independence. But along with freedom from colonial rule came the problems of socio-economic development and nation-building. Development had become the dominant issue in these countries, which came to be collectively known as the Third World. The concept of "Development Administration" had become the buzzword not only in the newly emerging societies but also among the Western nations and the UN institutions and documents keen in giving them technical and financial aid to enable them develop. Since its emergence in the early nineteen fifties, the subject of development administration has undergone veritable changes culminating into the now universally accepted concept of "good governance", with "equitable development" . A number of strategies have and are being devised to achieve its goals not only by the developing nations for purposes of furthering development, but by all the countries of the world in pursuit of excellence in administrative performance.

The present study in essence is a brief, but a critical examination of the various changing paradigms of the concept of "Development Administration", and the administrative changes and reforms carried out in the developing nations. It analyses the role of state, public administration, public services, and the initial four decades of crises in the evolution of the conceptual framework of development administration. It examines the phenomenon of failed developmental goals, and the concomitant evolution of the new paradigms of sustained development, market economy, globalization and the impact of the New Public Management, in directing, managing and controlling the means used in and by the Third World countries to achieve development.

As the study is a theoretical conceptualization and analysis of future trends of "Development Administration" in the last more than half a century, the methodology adopted for this kind of research has been a survey and scrutiny of the available literature and resources in the shape of government documents, UN, World Bank and other international organizations' reports and studies, commentaries and writings of scholars and practitioners in the field in the form of books and articles, surveys of social science discipline undertaken by various national and international academic and research organizations like the Indian Council of Social Science Research, etc. The material so collected, has been analyzed, critically examined, and presented in the form of a systematic narration. An attempt has been made to arrive at some definitive conclusions about the trend in the changing paradigm of the discipline and to make its study relevant and pertinent to modern developments in the field. It is hoped that such study would be most topical and useful to the scholars, policy-makers, and practitioners of public administration, who are in search of new paradigms and tools for evolving new methodology to address the problems of the developing world.

The style of documentation and referencing used in this study is mainly based on the New Harvard Style of Notation and Citation, [Name of author(s)] within the text followed by year, and page numbers], and full references at the end in the bibliographical sources which is rather different from the conventional style of citation used in most Universities in India, but is more accurate and simple to follow. .

In writing this study, we have received invaluable help and suport from a number of teachers, scholars, administrators and policymakers whose debts we must acknowledge. First and foremost we are most grateful to Hon. Shri T.N. Chaturvediji, former Governor of Karnataka and Member of Rajya Sabha for the inspiration and constant pursuance we got from him to work all these years, and especially on this project.

We will be failing in our duty if we do not acknowledge our immense gratitude to a number of national and international scholars and academics, from whose works and reports we have freely borrowed and quoted in our research work. Works of scholars like, Professors G.F. Gant, Fred Riggs, Kieth Henderson, Hartmut Elsenhans, O.P. Dwivedi, Renu Khator, Kuldeep Mathur, Mohit Bhattacharya, S.K. Sharma, Keshav Sharma and others have been most helpful and inspiring.

We are indebted to various experts in the field of Public Administration, who have been a source of great stimulation, and on many occasions, have given us very fruitful advice to bail us out, when we got stuck in the complexities of the problems of "development". Professors O.P Dwivedi and Hartmut Elsenhans have been kind enough to spare some of their valuable time to talk to us on the subject in their various visits to India. We are also grateful to a number of policy-makers and officials in the Government of India with whom we have had the occasion of interacting and discussing the nuances of the subject, which had been very enlightening. Indeed we must also acknowledge the help and assistance received in various ways in the completion of the book from Shri B.S. Baswan, and Dr. Rakesh Hooja, the past and present Directors of the Indian Institute of Public Administration, New Delhi.

We. are thankful to Dr. N.K. Gupta, former Head of Department of Political Science, S.D. College, Ghaziabad, who has virtually helped us initially on the project. We are also grateful to the Heads and staff of the Libraries of CCS University, Meerut, Delhi University, Centre for Policy Research, New Delhi, and S.D. College, Ghaziabad for the facilities provided to us to carry out our the research work. To Mrs. Sunita Gulati, Dy. Librarian of the Indian Institute of Public Administration, we are immensely thankful for her sustained help, and the trouble she took in searching and digging out, and providing us the necessary source material in the shape of documents, reports, books, periodical literature, especially the various international and World Bank documents, reports, and articles from foreign and national journals, on which the present work is based.

We are most thankful to Mr. G.S. Bhatia of Deep & Deep Publications Pvt. Ltd., to have readily agreed to publish this book and bring it out in this fine shape. Needless to say that for all discrepancies and errors, that have knowingly or inadvertently crept in this book, we alone are responsible.

R.B. JAIN
ANUJ JAIN

Introduction
End of Colonialism and Emergence of Developing Countries

INTRODUCTION

At the end of World War II, the age of imperialism came to an end and a rapid process of de-colonization began. By early 1960s, many of the erstwhile colonial countries in Africa, Asia, and Middle East, had gained independence. But along with freedom from colonial rule the newly independent countries faced serious problems of socio-economic development and nation-building. Development had become the dominant issue in these emerging states.

These new states along with the formally long independent but still "underdeveloped" countries of Latin America, subsequently became collectively known as the "Third World". The states in the Third World present great diversities and contrasts in their social composition, patterns of government, economic growth and cultural traditions. Over the years, however, they have exhibited a number of common characteristics that distinguish them from developed countries. All of these states are caught in the process of critical and disruptive political and social change. They share common goals of nation-building, growth, equity, democracy, stability and autonomy, and are eager to establish political institutions capable of controlling the state's population, of mobilizing its human and material resources, and of coping with the strains of social, economic, and political challenges without abdicating the state's control and mobilizational role.

Among the various political institutions that were expected to play a significant role in achieving these common objectives, was public administration, and with it the whole of public bureaucracy was regarded as the key instrument to take these towards the goals of development and nation-building. Despite the unending controversies surrounding the models, ideological orientations, goals, and concepts of development, the experiences of most countries in the Third World has clearly established the widely accepted premise that without an adequate and competent administrative apparatus, modernization, growth and development are almost impossible.

In most of the African and Asian countries, the end of colonialism has brought about numerous changes in political and administrative environments requiring new norms and relationships between the citizens, administrators and political leaders. For example, the non-responsible character of the bygone era had to give way to a more responsible and accountable system. A change in the political and administrative culture was deemed essential for the success of developmental plans, community projects and policies leading to socio-economic changes. Despite the four UN development decades since the 1950s, most developing countries still did not have an administrative apparatus capable of meeting the needs of accelerated administrative development and its inherent consequences. In those countries where a modicum of administrative apparatus does exist, it has been dubbed out by scholars, political leaders, foreign and UN officials alike for its slothfulness, lack of will and commitment to reform, and lack of responsiveness to legitimate public goals.

However, such criticisms apart, little attention has been paid by scholars to the "calculus of pressures", faced by these administrations in their environments which makes them so "lazy", or "indolent", or "uncommitted". The success of public policies in developing countries does not lie in rationality or in a new breed of public servants alone, nor is it found in an exclusive attention to the adoption of new management techniques and emphasis on the marginal role of public bureaucracies, which nevertheless become critical. There are a number of other environmental, political and cultural factors, which promote or inhibit the performance of public administration in the Third World. The success or failure of developmental goals depends to a large extent on the complex interplay of such variables. Notwithstanding the different ideologies and the nature of politics prevalent in the countries of the Third World, an effective public administration and a competent public service have been regarded as determining factor for their growth. As one perceptive observer has put it. "Underdevelopment seems to go hand-in-hand with under-administration" [Tsantis, Andrews C. (1969), "Political Factors in Economic Development" in *Comparative Politics*, Vol. 2, No. 1 (October 1969), pp. 62-78.] The role of administration thus becomes more relevant in the context of these developing nations, where the governments have to continually evolve strategies to meet the growing challenges of new types of political and economic demands.

CHARACTERISTICS OF POST-COLONIAL STATES

A common feature that has dominated the counties in the Third World has been the "ideology of development" incorporating the social and economic progress which determines the boundaries of political and social action, without at the same time specifying the exact form of the machinery for either political or administrative action. However, public administration, especially its institution of public bureaucracy as an instrument of state action became the principal vehicle for the accomplishment of development goals in all the Third World countries. Concerns have been expressed about the prospective role of bureaucracies and the possibility that they may stray from their instrumental role to become the primary power-holders in societies. The political role of bureaucracy has been one of the principal issues of discussion in the context of many Third World countries, as it has been in some of the more developed countries.

The importance of public administration and bureaucracy for development has, however, been universally recognized in all these societies. The basic pattern of public administration has generally corresponded to their former colonial systems. The three states of the Indian sub-continent, India, Pakistan and Bangladesh, have inherited a British colonial system of administration as have some African states, Kenya, Tanzania, Zambia, Uganda and Botswana. Nigeria has also much in common with the states of the Indian sub-continent in respect of its administrative legacy. The important traits of colonial bureaucracy still dominate their administrative systems, which include centralization, hierarchy, the persistent of generalist administrators, and the attitude of civil servants, who tend to see themselves as a distinct, elite groups in society. The colonial version of British, French or any other system of administration was suited to the requirements of colonial governments: it was more elitist, more authoritarian, more aloof and more paternalistic. Many of these characteristics have permeated the successor administrative systems in the new states. Besides, because of the growing intervention of these states in most human collective activities and resultant public enterprises, the states of the Third World have found themselves deficient in skilled, technically competent and specialist manpower necessary for their development purposes, resulting in low administrative capacities.

EFFORTS TOWARDS INDUSTRIALIZATION AND DEVELOPMENT IN POST-COLONIAL STATES

The post-colonial states have been characterized by the attempts these countries have made towards industrialization and development, which also gave way towards increased administrative activities. All the ideologies of development adopted by the countries of the Third World, whether capitalist, socialist, communist, fascist or populist, are built upon the fundamental premise of mass mobilization *ad infinitum*. Many of the developing countries, which had adopted industrialization as their policy goals blindly and totally, have simultaneously resorted to high militarization based on borrowed capital, weapons, and technology, which had led to the emergence of large, expensive and corrupt administration, whether civil or military. The bureaucracy in state owned enterprises, multinational organizations and military organizations continued to function in the interest of what scholars dubbed as "neo-imperialism". The various agencies in themselves became a set of bureaucratic colossus, competing for the leading edge of national bourgeoisie.

In many societies, the marginalization of masses and the ascendancy of multi-national capital have linked the phenomenon of bureaucracy and under development to the periphery of global capitalism. The state apparatus in many societies continue to assist the global forces of exploitation and domination, and the perpetuation of underdevelopment. The international environment has emerged as a system of influencing not only the details of their implementation. The concomitant process of militarization not only adds to the size and scope of the functions of national bureaucracies, but also enhances the authoritarian rule of civilian bureaucracies, reducing the role of national political leadership. In many societies public administration with its important organ bureaucracy has become the mainstay for dictatorial regimes which needed to build authoritarian states, both civilian and military for their survival. With only a few exceptions, dictatorship had become the way of life in most Third World countries. The attempt to modernize through the process of industrialization induced governmentaliztion and militarization, which had mainly contributed to the creation of authoritarian bureaucracy in the Third World, particularly in most of Africa and South Asia of 1960s and 1970s.

Collectively, these so-called Third World countries as "developing areas" account for approximately sixty-three per cent of the land area and seventy-five per cent of the population of the earth. About eighty per cent of the Third World population live in poor nations and in abject poverty. By and large, these countries have embarked upon the path of nation-building, modernization, economic development and social transformation with varying degrees of success and are seriously trying to bridge the technological and power gaps between themselves and the rich, prosperous, and "developed" countries of the West.

As Heady has observed, "the word 'developing', referring to the countries that are undergoing this process of social transformation, seems preferable to such alternative adjectives as backward, poor, undeveloped, underdeveloped, less developed, emerging, and transitional, and even expectant. This profusion of terms has led to the comment that the terminology develops faster than do the developing countries." [Ferrel Heady, *Public Administration: A Comparative Perspective* (New York, Marcel Dwekker, 1984), p. 75]. We shall use all these terms as interchangeable in our chapters throughout the project.

CHARACTERISTICS OF THE "DEVELOPING" POLITICAL SYSTEMS

Scholars have been engaged for quite some time in devising a common terms of reference for comparing these wide range of political systems outside the Western world. Lucien Pye identified an exhaustive outline of some of the dominant and distinctive characteristics of the non-Western political systems : (i) non-differentiation of political sphere from social and personal spheres, (ii) non-orientation of political parties or groups to a distinct political arena or a particular political principles, (iii) political process being characterized by prevalence of cliques, (iv) political loyalty is governed more by a sense of identification with a concrete group rather than with professed policy goals, (v) the role of opposition parties dubbed as obstructive of progress and seeking to disrupt the progress of the nation, (vi) political process is fragmented and criticized by a lack of integration among participants, (vii) political process is characterized by a high rate of recruitment of new elements into political roles, (viii) there are sharp differences in the political orientation of the generations, (ix) there is little consensus regarding the legitimate ends and means of political action, (x) there is little divergence between the levels of information and knowledge through discussion of the masses, (xi) there are no sharply defined divisions of labour in any sphere of life, (xii) there are relatively few organized interest groups with functionally specified roles, (xiii) the national leadership have to appeal to an undifferentiated public, (xiv) the unstructured character of the non-Western political process encourages leaders to adopt more clearly defined positions in international issues than on domestic issues, (xv) the affective or expressive aspect of politics tends to override its problem-solving or public policy aspect, (xvi) charismatic leaders tend to prevail in non-Western politics, and their position is further reinforced because of problem of political communication, and (xvii) the non-Western political processes operate largely without the benefits of political 'brokers' and with a few exceptions, instability is the dominant feature of politics. [Culled from Lucien Pye, "The Non-Western Political Process", in Harry Eckstein and David Apter (eds.), *Comparative Politics: A Reader* (New York, The Free Press of Glencoe, 1963), pp. 657-65. Also see S.N. Ray, *Modern Comparative Politics: Approaches, Methods and Issues* (New Delhi, Prentice Hall of India Pvt. Ltd., 1999), pp. 259-61].

MODERNIZATION, DEVELOPMENT AND CHANGE IN POST-COLONIAL SYSTEMS

As is clear from Lucien Pye's analysis the newly emerging countries in their quest for stability had begun to embark on a path of modernization, development and change. Although political scientists and analysts have given different interpretation to these terms, but development continues to be the most commonly used of these terms, however, the degree of consensus on what development means. Lucien Pye himself has given ten different interpretations of the concept of political development. [See Lucien Pye, *Aspects of Political Development* (Boston, Little Brown & Co., 1966; reprinted Indian edition, New Delhi, Prentice Hall Inc., 1973)]. Later in late 1960s and early 1970s, various interpretations of the term 'development' were presented through the work of the dependency, post-industrial, and social systems delimitation theorists. The term 'political development' according to Huntington and Dominguez was sued in four different general ways: geographical, derivative, teleological and functional. [Samuel P. Huntington and Jorge I. Dominuez, Chap. 1, "Political Development", pp. 1-114, in Fred I. Greenstein and Nelson W. Polsby (eds.) *Handbook of Political*

Science, Vol. 3 (Reading, Mass. Addison-Wesley Publishing Co. 1975)]. The functional approach as understood is movement toward a certain type of political system, toward the politics "characteristics of a modern, industrial society". Four types of problems or challenges are identified which put an existing political system under such strain; state-building, nation building, participation, and distribution or welfare. This led Almond and Powell to conclude that political development is a cumulative process of "role differentiation, sub-system autonomy and secularization."

STATE ACTION—THE PRINCIPAL VEHICLE FOR ATTAINING DEVELOPMENTAL GOALS

Despite several misgivings, the developing countries continued to share a generalized consensus of the objectives toward which change and development should be directed. The twin goals of development are nation-building and socio-economic progress. Developmental aims and the urgency with which they were sought invariably meant that state action was the principal vehicle for achieving developmental goals. Neither any infrastructure nor any means were available for gradualness or for primary reliance on private sector, as was possible in Western developed countries. Although state was seen as the main hope for guiding the society toward modernization, yet paradoxically, however, such reliance was coupled with widespread political alienation and antipathy toward politicians. Politics was seen as agitational and remonstrative rather than constructive and responsible.

Political instability was another prominent characteristic of the developing nations. As compared to developed countries of the West, the typical situation in developing countries was one of political uncertainty, discontinuity, and extra legal change. Political leadership was also concentrated in a minute segment of the population in most developing countries. Whatever might have been the background of political elites in a particular developing country, it was almost certain to be out of close touch with the masses of the population. Imbalance in political development was another characteristic consequence of past events in the developing countries. The stability of the regime was heavily dependent on the loyalty and competence of the civil and military bureaucracies, giving these groups with a professional orientation toward government a uniformly influential role, and often making them dominant.

GENERAL CHARACTERISTICS OF PUBLIC ADMINISTRATION IN POST-COLONIAL STATES

Whatever may be the characteristics of political regimes—civil or military—the importance of public administration is almost universally recognized in all developing countries. Usually an effective bureaucracy is coupled with a vigorous modernizing elite as a prerequisite for development. It was unanimously held that administration had been a neglected factor in development and that the existing machinery for management of developmental programs was grossly inadequate. Five general features of administration were currently in vogue in countries of the world:

First, the basic pattern of public administration was imitative rather than indigenous. The colonial version of British, French or any other system of administration was suited to the requirements of colonial government rather than governments at home. It was more "elitist, more authoritarian, more aloof, more paternalistic". Remnants of these bureaucratic traits have inevitably permeated to the successor bureaucracies in the new states. [Ferrel Heady, *Public Administration: A Comparative Perspective* (New York, Marcel Dwekker, 1984), p. 282.]

Second, the bureaucracies are deficient in skilled manpower necessary for developmental programs. Despite the abundance of labour in relation to other resources, there is a shortage of trained administrators with management capacities, developmental skills, and technical competence. Given the disparity between minimum needs and maximum possibilities for meeting them, there is no short range solutions to the problem of administrative capacities in most new countries. [*Ibid*., p. 283]

Third, there is a tendency for the bureaucracies in developing societies to emphasize orientations other than production-oriented. Riggs refers to this as a preference among bureaucrats for personal expediency as against public-principled interests. [*Ibid.*] Corruption, on a scale ranging from payments to petty officials for facilitating a minor transaction to bribes of impressive dimensions for equally impressive services, is phenomenon so prevalent as to be commonly expected. [*Ibid.*, p. 284]

Fourth, as Riggs has pointed about there is a wide spread discrepancy between form and reality which he calls "formalism" [Fred W. Riggs, *Administration in Developing Countries—The Theory of Prismatic Society* (Boston, Houghton Mifflin Co., 1964), pp. 15-10]

And, *Fifth*, the bureaucracy in a developing country is apt to have a generous measure of Operational autonomy, as colonialism was essentially rule by bureaucracy with policy guidance from remote sources, and this pattern persists even after the bureaucracy has a new master-after independence. The political role of bureaucracy, however, varied from country to country which was related to variations in types of political systems among the developing countries. [Heady, *op. cit.*, p. 285]

Having discussed the impact of colonialism on the erstwhile imperial colonies, which became independent after Second World War and examined the nature of political system and the characteristics of public administration in the newly emerging societies, it is appropriate to analyze the concept of development administration and its various parameters, which forms the subject of next chapter.

2

Emergence of the Concept of Development Administration

As discussed in the last chapter and emphasized by Milton Esman, "the concept of 'development' denotes a major societal transformation, a change in system states, along the continuum from peasant and pastoral to industrial organization. The assimilation and institutionalization of modern physical technology are critical ingredients. These qualitatively changes affect values, behaviour, social structure, economic organizations and political process." [Milton J. Esman, "The Politics of Development Administration" in John D. Montgomery and William J. Siffin (eds.), *Approaches to Development: Public Administration and Change* (New York, McGraw-Hill Book Co., 1966, p. 59.]

The notion of "Development Administration (DA)" which is a post-World War II revolution within the discipline of public administration, aims to achieve these changes in the developing societies. In the last years of the decade of 1950s, the concept had become the buzzword not only in the newly emerging societies but also among the Western nations and the UN institutions and documents keen in giving them technical and financial aid to enable them develop. It was rooted in the belief that 'administration', fashioned differently to suit the needs of "development", is the key to bringing about speedy socio-economic changes. {Mohit Bhattacharya, *Development Administration* (New Delhi, Jawahar Publishers & Distributors, 1997), p. 1]. The concept developed in cold war era, and in most cases US sponsored and American scholars and others set out to prove to the Third World that social engineering, properly planned and administered could bring about radical socio-economic change without falling a prey to the communist influences. [*Ibid.*]

The colonial pattern of routine law and order administration along with the associated civil service system and work procedures was found unsuitable for the accomplishment of the global tasks of nation-building and development programs achievement, which were considered to be relevant only for perpetuation of a system of colonial domination. There was no accountability of the system either to the legislative bodies or to the representatives of the people. There was no obligation on the part of public administration to work toward agricultural or industrial development of the country or to remove glaring socio-economic inequalities or regional disparities or economic imbalances. The two major functions of such administrative systems were: (a) to maintain law and order in the country, and (b) to realize the revenues accruing to the colonial masters. The colonial public administrative systems were basically centralized, authoritarian and suspicion-ridden.

EMERGENCE OF THE CONCEPT OF 'DEVELOPMENT ADMINISTRATION'

As mentioned in the earlier chapter, as against the colonial administration, the contrasting feature of 'development administration' was its emphasis on 'management of development'. It signified a planned and continuous effort toward increased institutional and personnel capacity to accomplish the varied and changing goals of development through the formulation of appropriate "policies, programs and projects" and their successful implementation. The administrative process had to enlist popular support and participation of people towards these goals and policies and had to be ultimately responsible to public at large.

The field of "Development Administration", was given formal recognition in early 1960s by the Comparative Administration Group of the American Society for Public Administration and the Committee on Comparative Politics of the Social Science Research Council of the United States, when the intellectual foundation of the movement had been laid down, which gained momentum during the early three decades of the later half of the twentieth century. The concept of development administration has been almost exclusively used with reference to the developing nations of Asia, Africa and Latin America. The term was supposed to have been first coined by Goswami in 1955 and then popularized by Riggs and Weidner. The conceptual paradigm has been distinctively Western though. Two different yet inter-connected Euro-American traditions converge in it; one of these streams of administrative thought is the result of an evolving trend of scientific management started at the turn of the 20th century with the administrative reform movement. The second current is the somewhat newer trend towards national planning and government interventionism which emerged as a direct consequence of the Great Depression of 1930s, World War II and post-war reconstruction. Bretton Woods and San Francisco Conferences of 1944 and 1945 welded these two currents of administrative thought into a new synthesis, which gave it the needed fillip to the growing discipline. [See O.P. Dwivedi and R.B. Jain, *India's Administrative State* (New Delhi, Gitanjali Publishing House, 1985), p. 200]

INDUCED DEVELOPMENT AS PARADIGM OF "DEVELOPMENT ADMINISTRATION"

The inspiration for 'Induced Development' as an emerging paradigm of development administration was European reconstruction through Marshall Plan, which was aimed at providing massive infusion of foreign aid thus establishing conditions for rebuilding the devastated economies of Europe, and was intended to stimulate accelerated and sustained economic growth. In the Marshall Plan, reconstruction and development were seen as two sides of the same coin and were conceptualized almost interchangeably. The Marshall Plan became the prevailing model of Western development through aid. In fact the terms 'reconstruction development' and 'planning' became inextricably linked to foreign aid. [Dwivedi and Jain, *Ibid.*, p. 201]

At the same time, the emergence of two super powers with diametrically opposing economies and ideologies, co-existing in an uneasy climate of entangling mechanisms of collective defence characterized the new era—one of cold war. In the realm of international organizations, the creation of the United Nations, had a fundamental impact in changing the fabric of the international system. A number of functional areas of international co-operation and development, however, gave the organization a new direction—the promotion of change through multilateral technical aid and finance. Throughout the fifties and sixties, the developmental role of the UN as a dominant feature of the organization and its related programs and agencies, particularly in relation to the Third World had come into being.

CHALLENGES OF DEVELOPMENT

As development became the dominant issue in the Third World, the Western countries had to respond to its challenges in a number of ways. The foremost was to conceptualize the notion of 'development administration'. Writing in mid-ninety sixties Donald Stone defined it "as the blending of all the elements and resources (human and physical) . . . in a concerted effort to achieve agreed upon goals. It is the continuous cycle of formulating, evaluating and implementing interrelated plans, policies, programs, projects, activities and other measures to reach established development objectives in a scheduled time sequence". [Donald C. Stone, "Tasks, Precedents and Approaches to Education for Development Administration" in Donald C. Stone (ed.), *Education for Development Administration* (Brussels, 1966), p. 41, quoted by Dwivedi and Jain, *Ibid.*, p. 202.]

Later George Gant in his treatise on 'Development Administration' elaborated its notion to be characterized by its *purposes*, its *loyalties* and its *attitudes*". [George F. Gant, *Development Administration: Concepts, Goals, Methods,* (The University of Wisconsin Press, 1979)]. The purpose of development administration were to stimulate and facilitate defined programs of social and economic progress. "They were purposes of change and innovation and movement as contrasted with purposes of maintaining the *status quo*. In terms of loyalties, the bureaucracy had to be accountable to the people and not to any vested institutional interests, nor to any king or empire. In terms of attitudes, development administration called for positive, persuasive and initiative stances from bureaucracy. The traditional norms or forms of administration had to be replaced by flexibility and adaptability to changing needs and situations. The attitude of development administration was outward reaching and not inward looking." [Mohit Bhattacharya, *Development Administration* (New Delhi, Jawahar Publisher & Distributors 1997), pp. 2-3.]

Such characteristics of development administration emphasized the formal and technical aspects of government machinery. Developmental goals were assumed to be agreed upon by the local (and Western) elites. These goals were often referred to as "nation-building and socio-economic development". Swerdlow has identified two inter-related tasks in development administration: Institution building and Planning. [Irving Swerdlow, *The Public Administration of Economic Development* (New York, 1975, pp. 15-19, quoted by Dwivedi and Jain, 1985: pp. 202-03] Other scholars have outlined a number of other development-oriented activities such as the management of change, establishing an interface between the 'inner' environment and larger intra- and extra-societal context, [See J. Fred Springs "Observation and Theory in Development Administration", *Administration and Society*, Vol. 9 (May 1977), p. 15.], and the physical and human energies and information and their subsequent conversion into policies and actions.

Also development administration was seen as concerned with the will to develop, the mobilization of existing and new resources, and the cultivation of appropriate capacities to achieve the developmental goals. Thus development administration becomes an essentially action-oriented, goal-oriented, administrative system geared to realize definite programmatic values. Professor J.N. Khosla had remarked that "Development administration not only envisaged achievement of goals in a particular area of development by making a system more efficient, it must also reinforce the system, imparting an element of stability as well as resilience to meet the requirements of future developmental challenges. [J.N. Khosla, "Development Administration: New Dimensions", *Indian Journal of Public Administration,* Vol. 13, No. 1 (1967). See also Dwivedi and Jain, 1985, pp. 202-3].

ADMINISTRATIVE MODERNIZATION THROUGH INDUCED DEVELOPMENT

Marshall Plan and reconstruction of Europe furnished a crucial lesson for the Western Nations that recovery of nations and development could be dramatically accelerated through improved management and organization. Such experience could also be used to suit the specific developmental needs of the post-colonial world. In fact, development administration was seen as a mutation of colonial administration by injecting development goals and structures into the old core of civil servants. The task of the developed countries was perceived as creation of *external inducement to change* through technical assistance and transfer of technology and institutions. [Ralph Braibanti, "Transnational Inducement of Administrative Reform: A Survey of Scope and Critique of Issues in Montgomery and Siffin (eds.) (1966), pp. 133-83, Quoted by Dwivedi and Jain (1985), p. 203.]

The crucial element in the process of "induced development" was the input of foreign expertise and capital (either in the form of aid or investment). A number of techniques such as program planning, community development and personnel management popularized during this era reflected the bent for external inducement towards modernization and westernization. This kind of approach operationally meant technological and institutional diffusion from the developed towards the depressed, devastated or underdeveloped regions. The diffusion of such an expertise was perceived as being value free and culturally neutral, and was supposed to have given the same results as those obtained in the developed world.—administrative efficiency and increased rationality. The more "developed" an administrative system became the greater the likelihood that it could have developmental effects. [Dwivedi and Jain, (1985), p. 203.]

The First three Decades of Development

The first development decade can be traced back from the 1950s with the initiation of the US President Truman's Point Four Program and the Colombo Plan, although from the UN viewpoint it began from 1960. As Dwivedi put it, "this was a decade of optimism, expectations, and the establishment of international aid agencies in various industrialized countries. It was also an era of general prosperity and also one of pervasive intellectual optimism throughout the world." [Dwivedi, O.P. (1994), *Development Administration: From Underdevelopment to Sustainable Development* (New York, St. Martin's Press Inc.), p. 8.] It was thought that with sufficient foreign aid and a revamped administrative system, Third World countries would follow the industrial and technical levels of the West. There was confidence that an administrative state would triumph with the help of new tools of development administration. "Administrative and military modernisation—both closely related developments—became the operational mechanisms for the preservation of post-colonial western ascendancy over the developing areas. But the expected administrative paradise did not materialize." [Dwivedi, *Ibid.*]

Further changes in this development paradigm took place with the beginning of the 1970s. The crisis of development administration in this decade came to unfold because of its inherent inadequacies. The issues of identity and purpose had devastating effects on the entire field of public administration, both developed and the underdeveloped world. After the accelerated growth of the 1960s, development administration seemed to have plunged into the "depth of intellectual depression". The development decade of the 1960s lost its impetus and a spirit of frustration and despair with development administration and with development in general had set in. It was quite evident by now, that despite its initial successes externally induced modernization had failed to eradicate the basic problems of underdevelopment which it purported to solve. Despite some increases of GNP in some places, poverty, disease and hunger had either worsened or remained unaltered. There was also the growing gap between the rich and the poor, and between different social strata within nations. Over administration in many countries was neither an efficient nor an effective insurance against revolution.

THE TWO ALTERNATIVE DEVELOPMENT PARADIGMS

The West was also facing several crisis of urban decay, social upheaval, protests and a deep questioning of institutions. Instead of affluence, growth and optimism, the administrative environment was being increasingly characterized by scarcity, decline and lowered expectations. Two basic trends emerged—one that the international and domestic development efforts had proven less than impressive and second, the failure of development and reformist concepts in general resulted in an expanding void.

At the beginning of 1970s, development could no longer be taken for granted and trend towards decay had begun to appear. Many events like the energy crisis, the growing economic recession in the major industrial countries, and a crisis of liberal democracy in the following years curbed most traces of earlier optimism. An increased contradiction between market economies and market policies appeared which had its roots in continuous economic growth to reduce social conflicts. Its consequences in the form of fiscal crisis of the state and a manifest trend towards stagnation and political stalemate constituted a new context for public administration.

The most severe intellectual crisis in development administration was the collapse of development theory. Serious controversies emerged about the manifest developmental failures of the decade, and a number of entirely different conceptions of development, produced mostly by scholars in the Third World emerged. The alternative developmental theories questioned the purported value-free stance of conventional development. The two identifiable theoretical trends came to be known as traditional and radical. While for traditionalists, development still meant economic growth, the radicals begun to define it in terms of human values, quality of life, distribution, satisfaction of basic needs, etc. Development 'for what', 'to what' and 'for whom' were not merely theoretical questions, but they entailed primarily normative consideration and value choices. The considerations of development moved from merely economic growth to human development as a whole and the fundamentalist conception of 'development as liberation' [Goulet, Denis (1973), *The Cruel Choice, A New Concept in the Theory of Development* (New York, Athenaeum), pp. xii-xxi, quoted by Dwivedi, *Ibid.*, pp. 11-12.]

Dwivedi summarises: "The failure of development administration strategies was a consequence of various factors. The tension between development administration, which emphasised mobilization, and administrative development, which was centered in the capacity for social control, lay at the core of its failure. Nevertheless, the crisis suffered by the discipline was not severe enough to make it disappear altogether." [*Ibid.*, p. 13.]

DEVELOPMENT: THE FOURTH DECADE—1980S—THE NEW INTERNATIONAL ECONOMIC ORDER (NIEO)

As we have seen above the 1970s witnessed an increasing gap between the centre and the periphery and the dependency theorists were questioning the very basis of the paradigm of development. Instead of development and nation building, turmoil and fragmentation were the order of the day throughout Africa, Asia, Latin America, the Middle East and in all countries of the developing world. All these had a dampening effect on the early optimism about the ability of First World administrative technology to solve problems elsewhere.

During the 1980s, in the Fourth Development Decade, the New International Order (NIEO) became an important new symbol in the development arena. "Its demand for a basic realignment economy, through changes in trade, and technological transfer", was appreciated, but generally ignored by the richer donor nations. There was in fact no global consensus concerning NIEO objectives, and some analysts felt that it might even harm certain countries. The NIEO represented a basic need strategy attempting to redirect the terms of development debate. While the World Bank and the International Labour Organization (ILO) somewhat endorsed this approach to development, the massive change in the world system demanded by the NIEO did not occur, and the NIEO also went the same way as the other concepts which had emerged earlier.

Another important factor that had emerged which was responsible for broadening the scope and spectrum of Third World problems was the collapse of the Soviet Union and Eastern European communist states, and the entry of some of them, especially in Central Asia, into the realm of the Third World. The orientation in these newly independent states was very much *pro-status quo*. A development creed soon emerged which posited that in order to attain development, a country's administrative structure should conform to the standards of the most advanced industrial societies. The key issue, then was the transformation of the existing traditional machinery into the new entity. This was to be accomplished through administrative development: the modernization of the public service machinery through external inducement, transfer of technology, and training by foreign so-called experts. While external sources placed a great insistence on sustaining these values in the Third World, in reality these principles were supplemented by existing traditional methods. Thus a parallel value system gained currency; western models were set-up and existed simultaneously with the traditional economy and black market. Rarely were the principles of development administration, as recommended by the experts from the West were questioned; as a matter of fact, these were generally accepted at face value by native elites, especially where relatively sooth transition to nationhood took place. [Dwivedi, 1994, p. 15].

The decade of 1980s marked the emergence of administrative systems that tended to be imitative and ritualistic. Practices, styles and structures of administration generally unrelated to local traditions, needs and realities succeeded in reproducing the symbolism, but not the substance. Yet at the same time a massive dose of political interference in the way of doing things stifled development initiative. The ineffectual developmental was to call for even more administrative development. Administrative reorganizations and reforms for the sake of abstract principles soon became the ends rather than the means of development administration.

In mid-1980s, it also became fashionable to talk about the 'Chinese model' and its emphasis on basic needs as an alternative paradigm of developmental goals. "The partial incorporation of the rhetoric of the model has often resulted in an idealized, distorted, and trivalised representation of an extremely different experience" [Dwivedi, 1994, p. 16].

Another crucial development in this decade was the disillusionment when the developing nations found that instead of being recipient of capital from the West, they were forced to make transfers of their meager resources to the West. In order to service their debts several developing nations became virtually bankrupt. Many African and Asian nations were beset with starvation, destitution, inequality and oppression . The golden age of the 1950s had turned into the age of pessimism and disllusion by the 1980s.

CONCLUSION

The above brief survey of the developments of the first Four Development Decades indicates that until this time the emphasis has been on modernization through the transfer of technology, and expertise from the Western world., which did not produce the desired and expected results for the developing nations. Thus a change of focus and strategy to include such key goals as sustainable development, human resource development, empowerment of specific groups, and removal of poverty, was necessary in the coming decade of development. In order for development administration to provide the impetus for the achievements of these core objectives effectively and forcibly, development administration had to be accountable, value-laden and relevant to cultural traditions. How have such goals affected the evolution of development administration will be examined in the following chapters.

3

Sustainable Development, Structural Adjustment and Globalization

Impact on Development Administration

INTRODUCTION

At the 1972 Stockholm Conference, Environment became an issue for international concern and action. Concrete policy statements on sustainable development and saving the world from further environmental degradation and working towards sound environmental management. As a consequence, The World Commission on Environment and Development produced the Brundtland Report (1987), which prepared the grounds for the Earth Summit of Rio in 1992, known as UN Conference on Environment and Development. The Rio Conference called for a new paradigm shift in 'development' and recommended that henceforth environmentally sustainable development should become the rule in all development strategies, projects and schemes.

SUSTAINABLE DEVELOPMENT : THE CONCEPT

The Brundtland Report defined the concept of 'sustainable development' as "development that fulfils the needs of the present without compromising the ability of the future generations to meet their needs." This obliges the humanity to use the resources of the planet earth in a way not to overuse them in the interest of posterity, as the indiscriminate over consumption by the elite and the affluent has been responsible for eco-destruction and planetary disequilibrium. There has thus been an all round realization that the consumerist model needs to be radically moderated and there is a lot that one can learn from the practices of traditional folk societies in respect of wise and balance resource use. To use resources and at the same time, not to over utilize them in the interest of posterity has been found to be deeply entrenched in the folk psyche. Forest, water, soil, crops—the natural resources have been maintained by folk societies as a matter of folk science or indigenous knowledge born out of actual life experiences. [Special Issue of *Development and Change* on "Development and Environment Sustaining People and Nature", January 1994, edited by Dharam Ghai].

Local resource conservation studies point out that the so-called 'development' from 'above' has actually meant deprivation from 'below'. People at the grassroots level are more and more marginalized and rendered poor by grandiose project like a big dam or a defence installation. From an environmental and social perspective, the current patterns of development are seen as resulting not only in ecological devastation but also in violation of property rights, displacement of people and the loss of livelihood and the way of life of entire communities. "Sustainability", it has been bluntly observed, "in the lexicon of the West now means sustaining Western privilege. This means preserving a form of wealth creation that diminishes us and tears humanity apart by the monstrous inequalities it imposes, at the same time as it culls the forest and mines the oceans, guts the earth and extinguishes civilizations, destroying all value and values but those that can be measured in money". It is in this context that rumblings can be heard at the grass roots level rebutting the repressive state politico-administrative discourses of this elite. [Quoted by Mohit Bhattacharya (1997), *Development Administration* (New Delhi, Jawahar Publishers), p. 83.]

The UN Research Institute for Social Development, initiated a research program in 1988 on Environment, Sustainable Development and Social Change, intended to investigate the social dimensions of environmental degradation and regeneration with special reference to the diverse and complex interactions between people and the environment. The underlying assumption of the program is: "programs and projects concerned with conservation and sustainable development will succeed on any scale when they address the social factors influencing the way people interact with the environment." [Dharam Ghai (ed.), 1994, *Development and Environment : Sustaining People and Nature,* Oxford, Blackwell Publishers, UNRISD. Quoted by Bhattacharya, *Ibid.,* pp. 84-85.]

Thus development from below, in practical terms means acknowledgements of indigenous knowledge systems about local situations and interest, local capacity to grapple with local problems. It has been said by observers with long-term local involvement in local development that local knowledge is bound by space and time, contextual and moral factors; and traditional knowledge systems were embedded in the social cultural and moral milieu of their particular community. [Agarwal, Arun (1995), "Dismantling the Divide between Indigenous and Scientific Knowledge," *Development and Change,* July 1995, quoted by Bhattacharya, p. 85].

Although the international and national contexts are not quite conducive for grass-roots participatory development, the World Bank sponsored structural adjustment program, to which we shall turn later is also not in any way concerned with participatory. On the contrary as has been pointed out "public sector development efforts, consisted in practice, largely of bureaucratic and technocratic approaches to the implementation of projects and programs much more than the people at the grass-roots. And in turn, these differential benefits strengthen the financial and social power of those same powerful interests, which enables them further to appropriate social resources to augment their private fortunes." [Quoted by Bhattacharya, *Ibid.*, p. 88].

Thus a new concept of 'sustainable development' is becoming a new paradigm in the global study and practice of public administration is, which by various definitions refers to global equilibrium, environmental sustainability by all governments, peoples and institutions, around the world. A holistic approach to sustainable development requires both the developed and developing nations as having responsibility for maintaining both a balance for survival and growth of their citizens. There is a growing understanding that development administration is not exclusively related to developing nations. Rather development is a universal phenomenon and all countries, including advanced ones, are engaged in development administration in a variety of areas. Thus, development administration and for that matter public administration as a field of study will be both global and comparative in the future [(Farazmand, 2001; Riggs, 1998, quoted by Jain, R.B. (2007), *Governing Development Across Cultures* (Barbara & Budrich Publishers, Germany)].

As Professor Khator has so rightly argued "to better understand the objectives of sustainable development, it is helpful to examine the characteristics that distinguish "development" from "sustainable development," (Khator, 1998, 1788-89). Sustainable development is distinct from development in its emphasis, scope, political sphere, cultural context, decision-making system and accountability. It is holistic, comprehensive, active, engaging, participatory and responsible." The distinction and transformation in the evolution of the concept of development is very appropriately depicted by Khator (*Ibid.*) through the Table 1.

In the process, while development administration remains an important sub-field of comparative public administration research, as was the case during the 1950s and 1960s, but apart from the quasi-normative nature of much of this research—the notion that the West should export their administrative systems to the third-world countries—has almost become redundant. (Pierre, 1995, 9).

TABLE I

From 'Development' to Sustainable 'Development'

Characteristic	*Development*	*Sustainable Development*
Emphasis	Economic	Comprehensive
Scope	Developing Countries	All Countries
Political Sphere	Neutral	Active and Engaging
Cultural Context	Neutral	Difference preclude replicability
Operational Mode	Unilateral transfer of knowledge	Bilateral transfer of lessons
Decision-making System	Centralized Administration	Decentralized Administration
Non-governmental Involvement	No role of non-governmental actors	Dependent on non-governmental actors
Role of Foreign Aid	Aid is a privilege	Aid is a responsibility
Accountability	No accountability	Accountability to people and to the international community

Source : Khator (1998, 1788-89).

THE DECADE OF 1990s : STRUCTURAL ADJUSTMENT AND AFTER

The early 1990s saw the emergence of a newer approach, sanctioned by the World Bank, IMF, US Agency for International Development (USAID), the British Overseas Development Agency (ODA) and other similar international aid agencies, which appeared to provide an alternative model to the cluster of problems associated with administered development, through "de-administered" development. The market-friendly policies championed by the Reagan-Bush administration in the United States, Margaret Thatcher's conservative government in England, Brian Mulroney in Canada as well as by numerous other West European Governments came to be universally applied.

The World Bank and other aid donor agencies made it conditional for the countries to adopt structural adjustment policy changes by downsizing bureaucracy, elimination of subsidies, and acceptance of devaluation in order to obtain aid for development. The most important policy step was to phase out or abolish the bloated public or state enterprises which were more of a drain on than assets for public resources. In some countries they had been over the years become a bastion of patronage, terrorized by powerful unions and scarcely producing quality goods or rendering quality services. A number of political and financial scandals came out on surface in Southeast Asian and Latin American patterns of business ownership by top level government officials and their families, and the opportunities for graft when private interests over public gain control over public sector operations; the power of enclaves such as drug cartels operating outside the normal governmental channels; and the coalitions formed between indigenous elite and multinational corporations. All these developments pointed towards the need for radical departure from the existing policy framework of development. Thus new structural adjustments programs like, government downsizing and reorganization became the new focus for development administration in most developing societies

Simultaneously some indigenous approaches, such as small-scale industrial organizations in China, or cottage industries development and Panchayati Raj system in India, Grameen-Bank in Bangladesh, and participatory 'bureaucratic' populism types and community-based decentralized structures for development came in operation which were regarded as alternatives to the traditional Weberian hierarchical administrative systems for development.

The New Strategies of Development : Decentralization, Public-Private Partnership

The new environment of structural adjustment emphasized market economy, public-private partnership and market-friendly strategies for development, which meant that government servants would have the need to reorient themselves towards a new and a more facilitative role. Much attention was to be given by public administration specialists to systems approaches and management information computerized systems, which in developing countries required detailed analysis of operations, with some important cautions regarding the pitfalls as well as the opportunities in their use.

The New Breed of Development Cadres

All these developments have had some effect on the role, task and training of the new development cadres. A new scientific and technological system for the creation and the expansion of appropriate administrative know-how was needed. If development administrators were to be some sort of new entrepreneurs, a number of formative conditions along the lines of the paradigm outlined earlier must be met. In operational terms, this entails the necessity to combine techniques with training in those social sciences which analyze and act upon the environment [Dwivedi, 1994, p. 32].

The new Administrative Cadre for development must combine appropriate administrative technology oriented to two types of clientele. The first is for grass-roots organizations involving simple technical know-how for management for change and problem-solving and for technical college and undergraduate level. Efforts in both sectors aim at the formation of a cadre of technicians able to see problems in perspective and apply basic management and organizing skills to concrete and specific questions. Secondly, there is also a need to prepare a fully-fledged professional—a tactical analyst—capable of understanding and acting in conjunction with the public sector. Thirdly, it is also important to see an academic cadre of 'strategic thinkers'. It is at this level where research and theorizing in the field must take place. In addition to these levels, it is necessary to establish the linkage between professionalism and the improvement of management for change capabilities.

The issue of improving managerial capabilities is not necessarily synonymous with the professionalisation of the public service. Managerial skills involve much more than the sort of general administration which used to be the trademark of colonial administration. The desired goal in most general terms is to produce competent, effective, responsible and ethical development administrators [Dwivedi, O.P. (1983), "Ethics and Administrative Responsibility", *Indian Journal of Public Administration*, Vol. 29, pp. 504-17.] The development of these skills also means improving standards and requisites of performance in handling developmental tasks. Public confidence and trust require that these managers maintain the best possible level of technical and moral performance, as well as a perceived dedication to achieving national as opposed to purely professional aims.

As Dwivedi has advocated, "Transfer of management technology is crucial for the Third World Nations, especially as they try to reduce their public bureaucracy under pressure from the North as well as from the international aid agencies. However, the most effective transfer in the management know-how will be when an indigenous, self-reliant capacity is created. This will be the challenge for both the North and South during the next decade or so. [Dwivedi, 1994, pp. 34-35.]

CHALLENGES TO DEVELOPMENT ADMINISTRATION AT THE THRESHOLD OF 21ST CENTURY

From the above discussion it is clear that development administration has faced a number of challenges at the beginning of the 21st Century. Over the years in the decades of 1980s and 90s there has been a growing political sophistication of the public, which has seen radical changes in the political and economic process. The public's sense of cynicism about the ability of those who govern and administer, particularly about the promises made by politicians, has made it more mature with respect to what to expect from those who govern.

There has been in recent years growing influence of religion and traditional values in politics and administration. Religion, casteism, religious fundamentalism have emerged as forces to be reckoned with and dealt effectively if the progress of development is to be maintained. In many cases these traditional values are at odd with western style development, secular politics and administrative efficiency. Religious fundamentalism not only gets reflected in political processes but also in the style of administration. These tensions and conflicts should be appreciated so that the demands of fundamentalism and the role of religion are accommodated within the needs of development administration. [*Ibid.*, pp. 45-36.]

Development Administration today also faces another type of challenge—the politics administration dichotomy or liaison? The concept of development administration as advocated by the West assumed many Western values including the separation of politics from administration. This type of separation was not embedded in theory and practice of development administration in many developing countries, as political factors did dominate the economic, social and administrative concerns. Most of the developmental issues are political as they deal with the authoritative allocation of values in the context of limited and sometimes fast diminishing resources. In developing countries, public administration could not have and still not purely within the domain of a value-free administration. Thus what is presently needed is a new style of public sector management, which blends the political, economic, administrative, cultural and religious forces to produce the desired results.

Another challenge faced by development administration today is the scarcity of new development managers. In most developing countries till now training of development administrators received a low priority in the planning process. Thus as a result the gap between planning and implementation grew, because of the institutional gap in the developmental process due to the underdevelopment of administrative and managerial skills.

Another trend witnessed in the last two decades, that culminates into challenge for development administration has been the declining standards of conduct and probity both among politicians and the civil services. The media continues to project a negative image of bureaucracy as being bloated, inefficient, status-conscious and authoritarian. The coming decades are going to be crucial for the Third World politicians and administrators, as they make efforts to uplift their people from the drudgery of poverty and malnourishment.

Thus ultimately the challenge before the leaders and administrators in the Third World countries is how to achieve the developmental objectives of basic human needs, that is the provisions of food, habitat, health and education, as well as social justice and self-reliance with limited resources at their disposal. The countries will have to be self-reliant while trying to augment their own resources, as they cannot expect continuing aid from the donor countries as in the past in the cold war era.

CONCLUSION

The end of the 20th century has brought momentous changes in the world system having far reaching implications for the developing countries. The hitherto East-West divide, which some Third World countries were able to manipulate in their favor does not exist any more. The collapse of command economy systems of Eastern Europe and the Soviet Union has pushed them to a kind of restructuring of the economy which would be particularly important in administered development a key for strengthening institutions.

It is now imperative that the developing nations should work for the orderly functioning of their administrative systems. They can ill-afford another decade of stagnation and stifled growth and therefore have to devise some new strategies for development and economic growth by revamping their administrative systems in the perspective of the forces of globalization and the concept of "good governance".

Globalization and the Concept of Good Governance

Challenges to Development Administration

Despite the crises in the theory and practice of development administration that we discussed in the last chapter, and their differences, developing countries, in the past two decades, have been caught up in a process of drastic and rapid social change. As argued by Heady (2001:299), they are all in transition, no longer traditional and not yet modern, either as they view themselves or as others view them. He describes five general features of public administration that may be considered typical in developing countries. First, the basic pattern of public administration in these countries is imitative rather than indigenous. Second, the bureaucracies are deficient in skilled workforces necessary for developmental programs, particularly, the shortage of trained administrators with management capacity, developmental skills, and technical competence. Third, much of the bureaucratic activity is channeled toward the realization of goals other than the achievement of program objectives. Fourth, the widespread discrepancy and the gap between expectations and actualities is often masked by enacting laws that cannot be enforced and adopting personnel regulations that are quietly bypassed. Fifth, the bureaucracy in developing countries tends to have a great deal of autonomy modeled after the colonial rule with policy guidance from remote sources. This pattern has persisted even after the independence of countries and there are few mechanisms for checks and balances to ensure accountability of government agencies. [*Ibid.*}

For developing countries, public administration is the central pillar of national development. Thus, administrative reforms continue to seek to build institutional capacities for making and implementing effective public decisions. Under the current governance model, however, national development is a collective effort involving the full capacities of private and public institutions working in partnership. The processes, structures, approaches, and theories that served well for generations simply prove to be poor fit for challenges of new governance model (Kettl, 2001). Many economic, diplomatic, and military problems have slowly moved to *ad hoc* supra-national coalitions and international organizations. Kettl argues that these trends are changing the role of national governments and raising questions about their capacity to perform these new roles. For example, what is government's new mission, how does this affect the job of administrative agencies and their managers, and how do *ad hoc* and international organizations fit into the new puzzles of governance, are some of the questions. Kettl goes on to say that while the problems raised by these questions fit poorly into the last century's traditional theoretical patterns, the governance model has served to advance the public administration theory in a future direction and find new paradigms. [*Ibid.*]

I. IMPACT OF THE PHENOMENA OF GLOBALIZATION/LIBERALIZATION

The trend towards globalization/liberalization in the late 1970s and 1980s led to a widely recognized fact that the role of the state in the 21st Century must be to facilitate for the continued global deregulation of markets and the denationalization of economic activities, more reliant on the instruments and values of the market (Welch and Wong, 1998). It appears, then, as argued by Professor Soni [Soni, Vidu (2007), in Jain, R.B. (2007), pp. 51-52] that the increasingly competitive economy demands a more competitive state, willing to emulate management principles embedded in the private sector. It is important to ensure the state's obligations in this regard are not compromised as a result of its pursuit of a radically different objective. If the state is to do this effectively, it must embrace a new way of thinking and evolve to become leaner and more strategic. This New World Order is less dependent on state intervention and approach to and design of its governance responsibilities (Kettl, 1993; Peters, 1994). Globalization represents the growing integration of the economic, financial, social, and cultural lives of countries (Thomas 1999:5). Even though views differ on the causes and stimulants of the recent rapid globalization, what matters most is understanding the results of globalization in order to ensure an appropriate management of public affairs within the global context. However, evaluating the results of globalization is difficult because of a complex mix of elements and a continually shifting emphasis and unpredictability of future trends. To complicate matters further, globalization has received much criticism, occasionally expressed violently, as happened during international meetings in Seattle and Prague in 2000. The critics and protesters complain that free trade has to benefit all citizens, not just corporations. Activists, human rights advocates, and environmentalists protested that globalization has deepened problems, even destroyed lives rather than promote economic growth evenly (Buerkle and Friedman, 2001).

Globalization has acquired a generalized application in recent years. It is widely understood as the increased deregulation of cross-border activity in the areas of economics, politics, and socio-cultural affairs (Farazmand, 1999b). Because the most prominent transnational actors in globalization are often thought to be financial and corporate entities, a number of commentators associate globalization with trade, financial flows, and technology spill-overs. Such cross-currents have not only had the effect of broadening and deepening linkages between global financial and capital markets, but also nation-states. Political globalization on the other hand is characterized by increasingly more homogenous/uniform ideological approaches to and practices of democracy, the design and implementation of public policy, and governance roles for the state (Cooper *et. al.*, 1998). In the face of an economically deregulated world, the state will have to come to terms with abandoning many of its traditional functions and obligations to the public in favor of fostering an environment of mass deregulation and championing the cause of the market. In the Western democracies, the state is increasingly assuming the role of enforcers of the rules governing various public policy initiatives framed at supranational levels. [Soni, *Ibid.*]

II. THE PARADIGMS OF 'GOVERNANCE' AND 'GOOD GOVERNANCE' AND THE INTERNATIONAL DEVELOPMENT DEBATE

Governance Defined

The concept of "Governance" has emerged as a new important paradigm in the evolution of the theory and practice of concept of administration as also of development administration in the closing years of the last century. Keohane and Donahue (2000:12) define governance as "the processes and institutions, both formal and informal, that guide and restrain the collective activities of a group." They explain that government is the portion of the activity that "acts with authority and creates formal obligations, whereas, governance describes the processes and institutions through which social action occurs which might or might not be governmental. Pierre and Guy (2000:7) argue, "Governance is about government's changing role in society and its changing capacity to pursue collective interest under sever external and internal constraints." Governance has become a popular way of describing the links between government and its broader environment—political social, and administrative. They explain that it is also a way of capturing the initiatives that governments around the world have developed to shrink their size while struggling to meet their citizens' demands.

Hyden, Court and Mease (2004:15) argue that although there is a general agreement among the international development agencies about "governance as an activity aimed at steering societies in desired directions", these agencies have typically adopted the concept to suit their own programmatic needs. For example, the United Nations Development Program has adopted the definition of governance as "the exercise of economic, political, and administrative authority to manage a country's affairs at all levels" (UNDP, 1997). UNDP has described governance is described as having three major elements including economic, political, and administrative.

Emergence of the Concept of 'Good Governance'

As Professor Renu Khator maintains, it was the World Bank that made an early attempt—perhaps the first attempt—to formally define and apply good governance in a document entitled *Governance and Development* (World Bank, 1992). While discussing development, the document read, "good governance is central to creating and sustaining an environment which fosters strong and equitable development, and it is an essential complement to sound economic policies." The report recognized three distinct aspects of achieving good governance: (a) the form of political regime; (b) the process by which authority is exercised in the management of a country's economic and social resources; and (c) the capacity of government to design, formulate and implement policies to discharge government functions. Since the first element—the form of political regime—was outside of its jurisdiction, the World Bank focused exclusively on the second and third elements and promoted them through the most potent tool it possessed, the landing practices. Structural readjustment was one such practice that forced developing countries to liberalize their political and administrative systems. The inherent assumptions were, of course, that liberal democracy was the desired form of government and economic development was the desired societal goal. To implement its program of good governance, the World Bank offered a list of criteria (Blunt, 1995, pp. 5-7): political accountability, freedom of participation by all groups, an established legal framework based on rule of law, freedom of expression, a sound administrative system leading to efficiency and effectiveness and cooperation between the government and civil society organizations. [Khator Renu (2007) in Jain, R.B. (2007), pp. 112-13]

In recent years, the issue of "good governance" instead of mere "governance" has become part of the rhetoric of governing in developing countries (Zafarullah and Huque, 2001; Bhattacharya, 1998; Werlin, 2003; Leftwich, 1994; Minocha, 1997; Fukuyama, 2004; Hyden, Court, and Mease, 2004; Jreisat, 2002). Invariably, good governance in developing countries is associated with factors such as building institutional capacities, activating citizen participation in making public policies, and improving education and training of government workers. The establishment of good governance is expected to help resolve some of the problems affecting the progress in developing countries and lead them toward better circumstance. Among other things good governance is expected to streamline the role of government and public organizations. The process is aimed at achieving a wide range of desired outcomes beyond prevision of public goods and services to creation of a value system which includes a rule of law, political accountability, transparency, efficient and responsive agencies, a participative policy process, and free media. Many of the elements of good governance have been described by various titles, such as, managerialism (Pollitt, 1990), NPM (Hood, 1991), market-based public administration (Lan and Rosenbloom, 1994), entrepreneurial government (Osborne and Gaebler, 1992). In the last quarter of the 20th century, states across the globe have demonstrated a preference for establishing "good governance" interpreting the concept in the way it suited them. This trend stemmed from the identification of several problems that negatively affect the performance of public organizations such as bureaucratic inefficiencies, corruption and cronyism, political interference in public management, and violation of the rule of law and fundamental rights.

The evolution of the various interpretations and transformation of the concept of development administration since the early 1950s to the beginning of this century has been very succinctly described graphically by Professor Vidu Soni through the following Tables 1 and 2 which summarize the

TABLE I
Governance and Development—Emergence of the Paradigm: 1950s—Present

Stages	*Focus*	*Method*
Post World War II democratization and decolonization of many countries in the continents of Asia, Latin America, and Africa 1950s-1960s	— Create a Nation identity — Nation-building — Institution-building — Industrialization	— Bilateral and Multilateral — Technical Assistance Programs funded by the U.S. and other Western countries
Emergence of Comparative and Development Administration 1960s-1980s	— Belief in scientific, technical, and value-neutral administration — Debate over striking a balance between universalism and separatism of administrative knowledge, structures and procedures across national boundaries	— Transfer of Western Administrative Models — Comparative information derived from study of cross-cultural administrative experiences and systems — Gradual internationalization of public administration, i.e., participation by scholars from developing countries in shaping the body of knowledge of the sub-discipline
Globalization and Liberalization Trends Post-Soviet Union Dissolution 1980s-90s	— Recognition of increasing global interdependence — Reduced role of the state as the sole agent of policy implementation — Development of democracy, economic development, and egalitarianism	— Deregulation of cross-border economic activity — Public-private partnership

Stages	*Focus*	*Method*
Governance 1990s – present	— Governance transcends the conventional boundaries of public administration. It is "the regularized, institutional patterns" that emerge from the interactions of public, private, and non-governmental organizations. (Hyden *et. al.* 2004, p. 13) — Simultaneous economic, administrative, and political reform — Development of effective public service and accountable public administration	— Redefining government's role as a facilitator rather than the sole actor in the development process — Increased reliance by government on non-governmental partners and markets to do its work. — Building networks and alliances among various societal institutions

Adapted from Soni (2007), pp. 80-81 in Jain (2007).

Table 2
Governance and Development (Adapted from Hyden, Court, and Mease, 2004)

Period	*Focus*	*Emphasis*
Phase I – Late 1940s—early 1950s	Project—Belief that good project design, without attention to the local context, was key to success. Projects constituted the means by which comprehensive national plans could be realized.	For the People—Development was a top-down activity by public agencies for the people. It was done on behalf of potential beneficiaries without their input. — Capacity building concentrated on the elites.

(Contd.)

TABLE 2 (*Contd.*)

Period	*Focus*	*Emphasis*
Phase I – Late 1960s	Program—Focus on designing integrated programs that addressed not a single dimension of human needs but the whole range of them.	Of the People—Development concentrated on adult education and universal primary education, i.e., development of the people was seen as integral part of poverty-reduction approach.
Phase I – Late 1970s-1980s	Policy—Strategic focus of development shifted to level of policy. The development burden no longer had to be born by government alone, but rather, must be shared with private sector and NGOs. — Implementation of structural adjustment and financial stability policies by World Bank and IMF.	With the People—People were no longer targets of development policies but rather partners that could be induced to make a difference for themselves and their country.
Phase IV – 1990s–present	Politics—Recognition that development is not only about projects, programs and policies but also about politics, in contrast with earlier view of development as apolitical. — Development needs a politically enabling environment in which people have a chance to create institutions that respond to their needs and priorities.	By the People—People, governments, constitute the principle force of development. They must be given the right incentives and opportunities not only in the economic arena but also political arena. — Thus, development is something done by the people.

Period	*Focus*	*Emphasis*
	— Development calls for reforms of the political set-up in individual countries. Therefore, the World Bank, IMF, and the international community have come to rely on the concept of Governance in which all major institutions of the society are participants in the development process.	

Adapted from [Soni, (2007, in Jain, pp. 80-81].

ideological, policy, and methodological elements of the stages of growth in governance and international development.

The stages, Soni maintains are not discrete, rather they describe the major trends in the development of the sub-discipline [See Soni, Vidu (2007), "Public Administration to 'Good Governance' in Developing Countries: The evolution of a sub-field in Political Science" in Jain, R.B. (2007), pp. 62-81].

After experimenting with different systems and models of public administration to achieve developmental goals, most developing countries are now in the process of formulating strategies to meet the challenges of 'governance' rather 'good governance'—the concepts that have become quite popular, as a result of the impact of, globalization, liberalization and of the New Public Management (NPM) movement of the early 1990s, coupled with the sustained efforts of the World Bank to pressurize the governments to undertake constructive reforms in their administrative system to fully achieve the benefits of the World Bank initiatives for development.

References

Blunt, Peter (1995). "Cultural Relativism, Good Governance and Sustainable Human Development", *Public Administration and Development*, 15.

Bhattacharya, Mohit (1998). Conceptualizing Good Governance. *Indian Journal of Public Administration*, 54(3): 289-96.

Buerkle, T. and Friedman, D. (2001). Globalization Foes Have Their Say. *International Herald Tribune*, (January 27).

Cooper, Phillip J. *et al.*, Eds. (1998). *Public Administration for the Twenty-first Century.* Orlando: Harcourt Brace College Publishers.

Farazmand, Ali (1999b). Globalization and Public Administration. *Public Administration Review*, 59(6): 509-22.

Fukuyama, Francis (2004). *State Building: Governance and World Order in the 21st Century*, Ithaca: Cornell University Press.

Heady, Ferrel (2001). *Public Administration: A Comparative Perspective.* New York: Marcel Decker, Inc.

Hood, Christopher. (1991). A Public Management for All Seasons? *Public Administration*. 69(8): 3-19.

Hyden, Goran, Court, Julius, and Mease, Kenneth. (2004). *Making Sense of Governance: Empirical Evidence from 16 Developing Countries*. Boulder: Lynne Rienner Publishers.

Jain, R.B. (ed.) (2007), *Governing Development Across Cultures: Challenges and dilemmas of an emerging sub-discipline in political science* (Ospladen, Barbara and Budrich).

Jreisat, Jamil E. (2002). *Comparative Public Administration and Policy.* Colorado: Westview Press.

Keohane, Robert O. and Donahue, Eds. (2000). *Governance in a Globalizing World*. Washington, DC: Brookings Institution Press.

Kettl, Donald, F. (1993). *Sharing Power: Governance and Private Markets.* Washington, DC: Brookings Institution.

Kettl, Donald (2001). The Transformation of Governance: Globalization, Devolution, and the Role of Government. *Public Administration Review.* 60(6):488-97.

Khator, Renu (2007). "Good Governance: An American Perspective in Global Context" in Jain, R.B. (2007), *op. cit.*

Leftwich, Adrian (1994). Governance, the State and the Politics of Development. *Development and Change*. 25: 363-86.

Lan, Z. and Rosenbloom, D. (1992). Editorial. *Public Administration Review.* 52(6): 535-37.

Minocha, O.P. (1997). Good Governance: Concept and Operational Issues. *Management in Government*. (October-December).

Osborne, David and Gaebler, T. (1992). *Reinventing Government: How the Entrepreneurial Spirit is Transforming the Public Sector*. Reading: Addison-Wesley.

Pierre, Jon and Peters, Guy B. (2000). *Governance, Politics, and the State*. New York: St. Martin's Press.

Pollitt, Christopher (1990). *Managerialism and the Public Services: The Anglo-American Experience*. Oxford: Blackwell.

Peters, Guy B. (1994). New Visions of Government and the Public Service. In Patricia W. Ingrahm and Barbra, S. Romzek, Eds., *New Paradigms for Government: Issues for changing Public Service*. San Francisco: Jossey Bass.

Pollitt, Christopher (1990). *Managerialism and the Public Services: The Anglo-American Experience*. Oxford: Blackwell.

Soni, Vidu (2007), "Public Administration to Good Governance in Developing Countries" in Jain, R.B. (2007), *op. cit.*

Thomas, Vinod (1999). Globalization: Implications for Development Learning. in *Public Administration and Development*. 19(1): 5-17.

United Nation's Development Program (1997). *Reconceptualizing Governance*. New York: UNDP.

Welch, Eric and Wong, Wilson (1998). Public Administration in a Global Context: Bridging the Gaps of Theory and Practice between Western and Non-Western Nations. *Public Administration Review*. 58(1): 40-49.

Werlin, Herbert H. (2003). Poor Nations, Rich Nations: A Theory of Governance. *Public Administration Review*. 63(3): 329-42.

Zafarullah, Habib and Huque, Ahmed S. (2001). Public Management for Good Governance: Reforms, Regimes, and Reality in Bangladesh. *International Journal of Public Administration*. 24(12): 1379-1403.

Reinventing Good Governance

Challenges and Strategies in India

INTRODUCTION

The advent of the 21st century has been characterized with the rising of poor quality governance and unsustainable development that has gripped the so-called Third World countries into a new form of mal-administration found rampant everywhere. A common feature that has dominated the countries in the Third World has been the maladministration of the existing political systems. Many of the characteristics of the colonial governments have permeated the successor states. In addition, because of the growing intervention of the state in most human collective activities and resultant public enterprises, the states of the Third World have found themselves deficient in skilled, technically competent and specialist manpower necessary for their development purposes resulting in low administrative capacities (Jain, 1989, 362-74). After experimenting with different systems and models of public administration to achieve developmental goals, most developing countries (including India) are now in the process of formulating strategies to meet the challenges of 'governance' rather 'good governance—the concepts that have become quite popular, as a result of the impact of globalization, liberalization and the impact of New Public Management (NPM) movement of the early 1990s, coupled with the sustained efforts of the World Bank to pressurize the governments to undertake constructive reforms in their administrative system to fully achieve the benefits of the World Bank initiatives for development.

I

CONCEPT OF GOOD GOVERNANCE

The term 'Governance' in its earlier interpretation was used to describe the 'activity of decision-making and the process by which decisions are implemented (or not implemented)'. However, it has now become a very fashionable and a broad concept, which is defined as the exercise of authority through formal and informal traditions and institutions for the common good. Governance encompasses the process of selecting, monitoring, and replacing governments. It includes the capacity to formulate and implement sound policies, and it assumes a respect for citizens. From this framework governance can be construed as consisting of six different elements. These are: (i) voice and accountability, which includes civil liberties and freedom of the press, (ii) political stability, (iii) government effectiveness, which includes the quality of policy-making and public service delivery, (iv) quality of regulations, (v) rule of law, which includes protection of property rights and an independent judiciary, and (vi) control of corruption.

Improving the quality of governance requires a system of checks and balances in society that restrains arbitrary action and harassment by politicians and bureaucrats, promotes voices and participation by the population, reduces incentives for the corporate elite to engage in state capture, and fosters the rule of law. A meritocratic and service-oriented public administration is a salient feature of such a strategy. However, synthesizing the strategy of key reforms for improving governance and combating corruption is a particularly daunting challenge, as is the task of detailing and adapting a strategy to each country-specific reality. Governance is more than fighting corruption. Improving governance should be seen as a process integrating three vital components: (a) knowledge, with rigorous data and empirical analysis, including in-country diagnostics and dissemination, utilizing the latest information technology tools, (b) leadership in the political, civil society and international arena; and (c) collective action via systematic participatory and consensus-building approaches with key stake-holders in society (for which technology revolution is also assisting). No two countries arrive at the same strategy, but to maximize the prospects of success, any country serious about improving governance for sustainable development must involve all key stake-holders, guarantee a flow of information to them, and lock in the commitment of the leadership *(Ibid.,* p. 6).

The World Bank has incorporated these features of quality governance in the concept of 'good governance' as "the one epitomized by predictable, open, an enlightened policy-making, a bureaucracy imbued with a professional ethos acting in furtherance of the public good, the rule of law, transparent processes, and a strong civil society participating in public affairs. Poor governance (on the other hand) is characterized by arbitrary policy-making, unaccountable bureaucracies, enforced or unjust legal systems, the abuse of executive power, a civil society engaged in public life, and widespread corruption."

II

CHALLENGES OF 'GLOBALIZATION' AND 'DEVELOPMENT MANAGEMENT' IN THE 21ST CENTURY

The threshold of the 21st century heralded the advent of the era of globalization. The politico-administrative system in India has to now face a number of growing challenges of the emerging phenomenon of globalization. In the coming years, there is likely to be a growing commitment to a free market and global economy, and therefore corporate governance is going to be a crucial factor in efforts to restructure governing institutions. With the end of the Cold War in the 1980s, the victory of capitalism, the emergence of new industrialized countries around the world and the new technological revolution, political, economic and social phenomena have in many respects bypassed the border of the state and acquired a global dimension. Under globalization, citizen demands are more diversified and sophisticated. They want choice, improved responsiveness and quality of services. With the diminished role of the state, a market-oriented economy supported by a democratic government with an efficient and quality-oriented public administration is conceived as the formula for economic development and well-being of the people. Privatization, deregulation, de-bureaucratization, and decentralization are the current political issues. Performance-oriented governance and management strategies are advocated to improve responsiveness and accountability. No wonder the concept of *development management*, which has gradually expanded to encompass bureaucratic reorientation and restructuring, the integration of politics and culture into management improvement, participatory and performance-based service delivery and program management, community and NGO capacity-building, and policy reform and implementation is increasingly gaining grounds especially in the context of developing countries (Brinkerhoff and Coston, 1999, 346-61).

Development management specialists now need to hone in on the critical managerial features of the problems that are preoccupying decision-makers and demonstrate how the discipline is relevant and useful. It is these decision-makers who must be convinced of the fit between development management and current global issues. Development management has made a difference in the lives of the citizens in the developing world, but continuing to contribute means remaining "in good currency". This is as much a challenge to the sub-field as renewing and advancing development management's practical and applied research agendas (*Ibid.*, 357). The policy-makers in India today face a real formidable challenge in striking this balance as a strategy for good governance. Given the present politico-social scenario of the country, will the system respond to these new challenges is a big question that is today agitating the minds of the policy-makers as also concerned citizenry in India.

The triumph of corporate millennium and world capitalism has led to a veritable tidal wave of economic and financial reforms in developing and transitional economies in the form of structural adjustment programmes. Coupled with the increased financial power of transnational corporations, the pace of technological innovation has led to an increased search for new products, new production methods and new markets. The revolution in information technology has not only made the world smaller but has also led to profound changes in the reorganization of production and industrial establishments. Both businesses and governments are under an intense pressure and scrutiny because people share instant information through a worldwide telecommunication network. There has been an expansion of world trade on a more competitive basis. The system of American dominated multinational enterprises is being replaced by a system of multinational alliances in airlines, telecommunications, banking, insurance, etc. At the same time the resurgence of massive international migration flows due to the global economic structuring, information and technological revolutions have caused worldwide demographic changes.

Along with the global transformation, the role of the state has been changing. The trend is to shift from a system where the state is the center of the world to a system where the territorial principle has to come into balance with the interdependency principle. The political power of the states has been weakened by supra-nations, sub-nations, economic forces, and macro-regions. In many countries, traditional bureaucratic public management is under severe criticism and is being gradually replaced by a new performance, result-oriented management along with efforts towards downsizing government bureaucracy, empowering local community, and encouraging private incentives. The tendency both at the national and local level is to evolve a common concept of governance implying a leaner, fairer and representative government, which allows for more individual freedom and active participation of civil society. Citizens are increasingly coming together and organizing to represent their interests, express their views, and undertake actions to assist themselves, either independent of or in partnership with government. In the globalizing world of the 21st century, the civil society takes on an increasingly powerful role in development and in influencing policies.

This rearrangement of roles, between the market, the state and people gives more space for the civil society to organize itself to effectively voice the interests of the people and of the common good. It also gives more responsibility to the civil society to take up the interests of the people whose voices would otherwise be overwhelmed and drowned by the powers of business interests of the politically powerful (Parr, 1997, 1-2).

The Pressures of Globalization

Contrary to widespread pessimism regarding the effects of globalization on nation-states and the quality of governance in developing countries in the present century, Professor Harald Fuhr in one of his contribution stresses—somewhat provocatively—that several of its features can be made instrumental, and be beneficial, in terms of improving public policy-making and state capability.

According to him, Four "constructive pressures" stemming from globalization could be seized constructively by citizens and governments in the developing world: *First,* better informed and better connected citizens, and an emerging global civil society, demand improvements in service delivery, transparency, and participation. *Second,* subnational governments, often backed by local NGOs and businesses, and keen to attract foreign investment, increasingly exert pressure *vis-à-vis* central governments. *Third,* global investment strategies by private businesses increase the demand for appropriate institutional arrangements within developing countries as well as credible government policies. Although with mixed results. *Fourth,* International Organizations, in particular IFIs, have been addressing public sector modernization in developing countries, also sponsoring global public policy networks in critical areas. Moreover, policy coordination and cooperation among states increases significantly, constraining arbitrary action by governments. Globalization, thus, advances the discussion about, and the demand for, new institutional arrangements, clearly with new opportunities for improvements in state capability and governance (Fuhr, 2003). How to develop these new institutional arrangements so as to increase the capability of the state and government is a major challenge faced by the political leaders and policy-makers in India.

III

INDIA'S EXPERIENCES IN GOVERNANCE AND ADMINISTRATIVE DEVELOPMENT

The threshold of the new millenium has furnished us with a good occasion to reflect upon and evaluate India's experiences in administrative development towards its pursuit of good governance and ponder over the likely emerging trends and the lessons learnt for the future. Reflecting upon the realities of public administration system in India over the last half a century is not a simple exercise, for India is a complex society composed of diversity of languages, social systems, ethnic, tribal and caste groups, various religions, regional disparities, different cultural patterns, and unlimited environmental factors that shape the behavioural pattern of masses and public functionaries at all levels, which affect the idea of rationalism in administrative behaviour. It is indeed very difficult to objectively evaluate the impact of all these factors on governance. The Government of India has since Independence in 1947 taken a number of steps to revamp the system of administration at different stages of its evolution with a view to secure objectivity, transparency, efficiency and responsiveness in the administrative process—the basic ingredients of good governance in a democratic system-based on the concepts of rule of law and public welfare.

As it appears, the search for the elusive goal of good governance in India has been simultaneous with the evolution of a constitutional democratic government—a government which is limited, stable and truly representative of the majority of the people, maintains its territorial integrity and national sovereignty, accelerates economic growth and development, upholds the rule of law and renders justice without fear or favour and without delay, and ensures welfare of all sections of the people. These objectives were sought to be achieved through the adoption of the Republican Constitution in 1950. However, despite the lofty ideals and the values of good governance enshrined in the Constitution, we find ourselves today in a state where the system has not been able to provide either a stable government or stable policies. What has gone wrong in our constitutional and administrative system during the last fifty years has been a subject of endless debate and discussions, and a number of prognosis have been made by constitutional and administrative experts, political leaders and policy-makers, various commissions and committees to reform and restructure the system to be able to achieve the objectives of good governance. "Has the system of government failed in India or the people have failed the system" is an oft repeated question being raised again and again without any satisfactory answer.

As was so emphatically suggested by the author elsewhere (Jain, 2001) that it is wrong to always blame the structural aspects of governmental system for our failures. Given the normal wear and tear in the edifice of the governmental and administrative system over a period of over fifty years, the system as a whole has not only survived, but also admirably borne the burnt of times, in comparison to the scores of examples of other countries in the developing world where such structures have crumbled completely.

However, at the same time a number of serious distortions have crept in the system during all these years, giving validity to the dictum of Woodrow Wilson that "it is easier to make a constitution than to run it." The foremost and fundamental reason for all these aberrations has firstly, been the existence of a dual system of values on the part of political and administrative elites in India, who have the basic responsibility of implementing the system. In their public pronouncements and external behaviour, they are highly idealistic and show deep concern for integrity, equity and justice—the prime values of good governance, but in practice, when it comes to actual decision-making and its implementation, the same political and administrative elites are vulnerable to all kinds of narrow prejudices, biases and pressures of caste, community or religion, or political compromises in order to continue to remain in power by all possible means—fair or dubious. This has been a marked trend in India's political and administrative development especially since 1960s. The public postures of political and administrative leaders hardly match their actual behaviour on the positions they hold and the values they espouse.

Secondly, there has been a growing sense of zealousness amongst the people from all walks of life in India about their constitutional rights and administrative privileges without paying due attention to the corresponding duties that go with them. The level of tolerance among the people in India, which was the hallmark of their social, cultural and political behaviour in the first two decades of the Republic seems to have lost somewhere in the labyrinthine of the struggle for power. People will go to any length of aggressive, unfair, immoral and unjudicial conduct to achieve their selfish goals. This general decline in standards of behaviour and conduct of mutual relations have been more prominent in the floors of our legislatures—once considered the temples of democracy. The honourable members of these august bodies increasingly seek to settle their individual and political scores by blocking their proceedings, creating pandemonium, showing fists, hurling shoes, chairs and microphones, and breaking the heads and teeth of political opponents. All these happenings have had some disastrous consequences for the social and political system as a whole. People in all fields of professions and occupations will go to any extent and resort to any form of agitations in demanding their rights, but would not care for the obligations that such rights carry. Whether it is the student bodies, the academics, the labour organizations, the business or industrial groups, there are agitations galore for all kinds of demands on the state and against any move of the government to bring about any reform or semblance of discipline in the system holding the citizens at large to ransom and throwing the daily lives of the people out of gear and at the same time putting strains and pressures on the performance of the system.

Thirdly, at the same time the total lack of a notion of accountability and responsiveness on the part of both our legislators and administrators has eroded the very essence of a responsible government. There are political rhetoric and polemics, but no substantial accomplishment in respect of the citizens' needs and aspirations. There are innumerable grandiose policies, plans, programmes and projects, which we are very apt to formulate, but no plans or will to implement these 4 ps. The result is either stagnation or a very slow growth in the realm of progress and development. On top of it, the bureaucracy in India is cold, slow and somewhat inhuman in dealing with the complaints of the citizens. Worst, it carries an image of being the most corrupt amongst the world bureaucracies. Instances of administrative excesses, police brutality, nexus between politicians, bureaucrats and the criminals for securing political and personal ends appear endlessly in the media practically everyday. Billions of rupees are being spent everyday on the security, privileges and 'welfare' of the politicians, legislators, ministers and other political and administrative functionaries, but without any proportionate returns on the welfare of the masses. There is an open exploitation and the use of money power, muscle power and mafia power all around for securing personal and material gains without the slightest qualms on one's conscience or on one's moral sense of responsibility for efficient and effective governance.

Fourthly, in India poor are still poor and have even increased in absolute numbers. Economic gains have been wiped out by population growth. Though India has an economically powerful middle class, a vibrant software industry, and nuclear capability, but a huge number of India's citizens continue to eke out a living under conditions of extreme poverty and deprivation. The government's capacity to perform is still weak, resources available for public investment and development are still scarce, local jurisdictions are particularly starved. The critical basic needs in education, health, welfare, infrastructure and the very basic need of clean drinking water for the masses still go unmet. Many of the poor are in fact worse-off now than they were a decade or so ago. No wonder that India ranks very low in the Human Development Report prepared each year by the UNDP. Human development is the strand which holds together concerns on political institutions and governance, social institutions and culture, and science and technology. Ultimately what really matters is how the interaction between globalization and these different institutions redounds to higher levels of human development.

As one of the observers of the Indian political scene has rightly put it "poverty is the biggest political constituency in India. Not only do our politicians feed-off it like vultures but supposedly pro-poor activists and NGOs also rush around condemning economic reforms on the grounds that the poor will not benefit.... A favourite whipping boy of the "pro-poor" activists is globalisation. This they tell us is definitely anti-poor but again they do not ask if globalisation is an option anymore or a reality we have to face. There are not many countries left in the world so over regulated as we are...there is much we can gain by learning from other kinds of systems of governance where we went wrong" (Singh, 2000; 26). What particular social and economic model can be devised at this juncture of the evolution of the Indian polity, with vociferous disruptive tendencies without any coherent ideological stance remains the biggest challenge for the policy-makers in India at the beginning of the millennium.

IV

DEVELOPMENT APPROACHES AND GOVERNANCE IN INDIA'S FIVE YEAR PLANS

Since the advent of planning in India in 1950, various plan documents have emphasized progress in different sectors of economy for promoting development and removing poverty in the country. It is only since the early 1990s that there is a change of emphasis on the perspective on development to include the concept of "human development" deviating from merely confining to socio-economic parameters. The Eighth Plan document stressed that human development will be 'the ultimate goal' for the period 1992-97, and 'employment generation, population control, literacy, education, health, drinking water and provision of adequate food and basic infrastructure' were listed as priorities. It was thus necessary that every effort should be made to mitigate the adverse impact of adjustment on the poor, both in the short-term and long-term (*Ibid.*, pp. 73-74).

Similarly, the Approach paper for the Ninth Five Year Plan, accorded priority to agriculture and rural development as a vehicle for accelerating the growth of overall economy which should encompass basic services such as safe drinking water, primary health care, universal primary education and shelter. Simultaneously, it should strive for containing the growth rate of population, people's participation at all levels, empowerment of women and socially disadvantaged groups such as Scheduled Castes, Scheduled Tribes, Other Backward Classes and Minorities. "Growth with Social Justice and Equity" sums up the goal set forth in the 9th Plan before the Nation. For eradication of poverty and unemployment, the strategy was to (i) accelerate economic growth with stable prices, since there was evidence to show that rapid growth had strong poverty reducing effects; (ii) focus on direct anti-poverty and employment programmes; and (iii) accord priority to governmental expenditure in social sectors (Government of India, 2000, 64).

The Tenth Five Year Plan Approach Paper aims at a sound policy of development by harnessing the human and natural resources of the country to enhance the quality of life and the well being of the people. It maintains that "economic growth cannot be the only objective for national planning and indeed over the years, development objectives are being defined not in terms of increases or per capita income but more broader in terms of enhancement of human well-being." It also emphasizes that "economic prosperity measured in terms of per capita GDP does not always ensure enrichment of quality of life as reflected, for instances, in the social indicators on health, longevity, literacy and environmental sustainability, etc." It also includes the expansion of economic and social opportunities for all individuals and groups and greater participation in decision-making (Approach Paper, 2001, pp. 2 and 49).

Although in the past ten years, the economic stabilization policies in India have worked quite well in turning around the balance of payments and producing quite comfortable foreign exchange reserves, but the size of increasing fiscal deficit is constantly worrying policy-makers. This reflects the fact that most public expenditure cuts were on developmental expenditures (including investments in agricultural infrastructure, rural development, energy, industries, communication, and science and technology) leaving less productive revenue spending (including interest payment, subsidies and civil service spending) more or less unaffected. The ensuing composition of public expenditures thus ignores the vital importance of adequate rural infrastructural facilities for future economic growth and poverty alleviation, while leaving many prevailing inefficiencies intact, thus endangering the sustainability of the noted achievements (Stuijenberg and Van, 1996, 31-89).

Governance Reforms Proposed by the Approach Paper to the Tenth Five Year Plan

Pointing out a number of deficiencies in the system of governance in India, the Approach paper to the Tenth Five Year Plan has noted:

> While the functions of the state in India have steadily increased, capacity to deliver has declined over the years due to administrative cynicism, rising indiscipline, and a growing belief widely shared among the political and bureaucratic elite that the state is an arena where public office is to be used for private ends. In almost all states people perceive bureaucracy as wooden, disinterested in public welfare and corrupt. The issue of reform in governance has acquired critical dimensions in poorer states in the light of low economic growth and fiscal crisis. Weak governance, manifesting itself in poor service delivery, excessive regulation, and uncoordinated and wasteful public expenditure, is seen as one of the key factor impinging on growth and development (Para 4.11, p. 45).

The paper emphasizes that the agenda of reform in governance should include not only reshaping the bureaucracy by adopting a comprehensive reform of civil services, and a multi-faceted strategy based on ensuring security of tenure, increasing accountability, civil service renewal, open and responsive government, tackling corruption and strengthening the rule of law, and e-governance (*Ibid.*, 46).

Similarly the Approach Paper to the XIth Five Year Plan emphasizes, "Good Governance and Transparency should be ensured in the implementation of public programs and also in the government's interaction with ordinary citizens. Corruption is now seem to be endemic in all spheres of life. Better designs in projects, implementation mechanism and procedures can reduce the scope of corruption. Much more needs to be done by both the Centre and the Stares to lessen the discretionary powers, ensure greater transparency and accountability, and create awareness among citizens. The Right to Information Act (RTI) empowers people to demand improved governance, and as government we must be ready to respond to this demand." (Approach Paper to XIth Five Year Plan, 2006, 1.6.16)

V

STRATEGIES NEEDED FOR GOOD GOVERNANCE AND SUSTAINABLE DEVELOPMENT

In the perspective of these developments world around and in India, the fundamental question that arises is to devise the strategies that would be conducive for the developing nations, particularly India, to strive towards sustainable development. Besides the institutional and structural innovations that make for a system of good governance, a corruption free sustainable development requires a "moral determination" (Dwivedi, 1987, 607-9 and 2001). Recognition of that moral determination in governance marks the direction in which those who govern must channel their efforts toward the common good if they are to justly serve the society. That direction calls for individual moral responsibility and accountability, sacrifice, compassion, justice and an honest effort to achieve the common good. Ultimately, it is the moral determination which provides the foundation for governance towards a corruption-free sustainable development.

(i) Adopting a Normative Model of Good Governance

Thus the need of the hour at present seems to be to adapt a normative model of *Good Management Approach* incorporating both the politico-administrative as well as the moral dimensions of good governance. This should, include: (a) A more strategic or result-oriented (efficiency, effectiveness and service quality) orientation to decision-making; (b) Replacement of highly centralized organizational structures with decentralized management environment integrating with the new Rural, Urban and Municipal Institutions, where decisions on resource allocation and service delivery are taken close to the point of delivery; (c) Flexibility to explore alternatives to direct public provision which might provide more cost effective policy outcomes; (d) Focusing attention on the matching of authority and responsibility as a key to improving performance, including mechanism of explicit performance contracting; (e) Creating of competitive environments within and between public service organizations; (f) Strengthening of strategic capacities at the Center to steer government to respond to external changes and diverse interests quickly, flexibly and at least costs; (g) Greater accountability and transparency through requirements to report on results and their full costs; (h) Service wide budgeting and management systems to support and encourage these changes; (i) The most important task to break the growing nexus of bureaucrats, politicians and criminals leading not only to a breakdown of the total system but also to a sense of cynicism amongst the citizenry; (j) Adapting of innovations and evolving suitable mechanism to eliminate corruption at both political and administrative levels and strengthen citizens' grievance redressal system; (k) Improving the system of delivery at the cutting edge of administration by replacing the existing archaic bureaucratic procedures by absorbing some appropriate precepts inherent in the philosophy of New Public Management; and (l) Making improvements in the working atmosphere of the government institutions and offices to reflect a new work culture and a changed administrative behaviour incorporating the principles of transparency, responsiveness, accountability, participative and citizen-friendly management.

(ii) The Public-Private Sector Synergy

There is no doubt that the process of globalization and the simultaneous rapid economic and technological changes have greatly affected the pattern of governance in modern times.

Scholars have argued that The actual pattern of governance in internationalized environments can be related to the respective governance capacity of public and private actors, which hinges in turn on the strategic constellation underlying the provision of public goods. The specific strategic constellations varies along three dimensions namely, the congruence between the scope of the underlying problem and the organizational structures of the related actors; the type of good problem; and the institutional context. For their part, each of these combines a number of factors (Knill and Lehmkuhl, 2002, 41-63). On the basis of this concept four ideal types of governance, enabled by their differing configurations of public and private capacities to formally or factually influence in various ways the social, economic and political processes employed in the provision of certain goods have been identified. Assessing the implications of economic and political internationalization on the governance capacities of public and private actors, internationalization has been described as a process in which the patterns of governance are transformed along three paths: from interventionist regulation to regulated self-regulation; from interventionist regulation to private self-regulation; and from interventionist regulation to interfering regulation. The analysis of the consequences of internationalization for the patterns of governance further suggests that the expectation of the weakening of the state, or a mutual driving out of governance activities of public and private actors can hardly be confirmed. The relationship between public and private actors is not free from conflict; neither is it paralyzed by conflict. In essence there is a dynamic, synergetic relationships, with public and private contributions reinforcing each other over time. However, such mutual dependencies between public and private actors and their concept to cope with specific problems are apparent only in the implementation of certain regulatory arrangements and do not take into account the problems related to accountability and the democratic legitimacy of regulatory structures. Thus a crucial question becomes important : how is it possible to ensure that private governance activities are kept responsive to wider societal interests? (*Ibid.*, 57-58). The question of accountability, therefore, becomes a key factor and an issue of good governance.

Now-a-days, a new model is also being discussed, called the Public-Private Community Partnership (PPCP) model, wherein both the government and private players work together for social welfare, eliminating the prime focus of private players on profit. This model is being applied more in developing nations as in India. Success is being achieved through this model too. it mainly helps to ramp up the development process as the focus is shifted towards target achievement rather than profit achievement. These not-for-profit organizations bridge public and private sector interests, with a view toward resolving the specific incentive and financial barriers to increased industry involvement in the development of safe and effective pharmaceutical and other types of products. (Wijkipedia, culled from Googles, 20 September 2010)

(iii) Accountability as a Basic Requisite for Good Governance

If the concept of accountability refers to the degree to which public servants and others in non-governmental sectors providing public programs are responsive to those they serve, then there is a need for multi-dimensional methods to measure how different institutional arrangements advantage different forms of responsiveness. The traditional measures of accountability that rely upon line or top-down measures do not necessarily provide a good guide to the accountability culture as a whole. As service delivery systems move to more complex forms of agency, accountability at other levels must be expected to undergo a dynamic process of evolution, adaptation, and in some cases—crises. It is clearly not enough to bemoan the decline of a parliament or the weakness of the consumer. Institutional development must fit each case. Vertical strength can be improved with stronger roles for parliamentary committees, ombudsmen, and so on. Tools for greater horizontal accountability will need to be different for competitive systems and for those using more collaborative methods. In both cases, a focus upon the role of reflexive feedback or improvisation offers a means to reopen the organizational process box without the perils of re-regulation. This new domain of accountability will take sometime to develop its own regime of measures, standards and rules. Perhaps the most important step needed is the recognition that multi-dimensionality of accountability means both multiple measure and new mandates (Considine, 2002, 21-40).

(iv) Adoption of IT and the Concept of E-Governance

The revolution in information technology has brought into focus its adoption for good governance. There is a talk of e-governance all over the world. E-governance implies a smoother interface between government and citizen. While it cannot entirely replace manual governance, even its limited applications are good enough to affect day-to-day living. It can fulfil roughly speaking, the four purposes for which citizens generally interact with the government : (i) paying bills, taxes, user fees and so on, (ii) registration formalities, whether of a child's birth or a house purchase or a driving license. (In Tamil Nadu for instance, one can download 72 application forms), (iii) seeking information, and (iv) lodging complaints. E-governance can reduce distances to nothing, linking remote villages to government offices in the cities, can reduce staff, cut costs, check leaks in the governing system, and can make the citizen-government interaction smooth, without queues and the tyranny of clerks. But it must be remembered that E-governance is only a tool for good governance. It can't succeed independent of responsive officers, and it has to be owned by the political leadership. Otherwise it will only be a bureaucrat's game (*India Today,* 11 Dcember 2000, 70-76, also see Jain, R.B. (2007), 1418-23). How to rebuild the system of governance on these new premises without the majority of population even being literate is a real challenge for all concerned with new innovations in the performance of the government in India.

Luo Xiao-hua in an Electronic contribution has subscribed to the fact that, [*http://doi.ieeecomputersociety.org/10.1109/ICMeCG.2009.96*]. E-governance initiatives are common in most countries as they promise a more citizen-centric government and reduce operational cost. Unfortunately most of these initiatives have not been able to achieve the benefits claimed. Often the reason for this failure is a techno-centric focus rather than a governance-centric focus. Therefore, the aim is to explore the necessary attributes of a governance-centric initiative under the banner "excellent e-governance", and describe a methodology for ensuring such excellence in e-governance implementations. There should be a case study approach for developing the concept of excellent e-governance. Thus a methodology, which may be called "e-governance engineering", should be develped, which when applied to an e-governance initiative, will ensure excellence.

(v) The Citizen-oriented Paradigm of Good Governance

The corporate millennium has brought into focus a new concept of governance based on the interests of the share-holders, i.e. the citizens, which has signaled the role of transparency, accountability and merit-based management and a sense of morality and ethics that rests on the principle of "concern for others." An ethical organization, more so a government not only stands for people with a set of values, but a positive attitude which generates a culture within the organization in which every member feels a sense of loyalty and belonging and the leaders are responsible for initiating dialogues across a wide range of levels and functions so as to operationalize values in practical policies.

Modernization of government and public administration involves a redefinition of government responsibilities. The state system of the 21st century, will have to see a redistribution of duties and responsibilities between government, business and society. The guiding principles is the idea of the "empowering state", which leaves more space for society and individual commitment. The internal structures of government administration should also become part of this developmental process. This would require introduction of modern management techniques with quality control, budgeting and cost-benefit analyses. In future, public authorities are meant to be results-oriented in providing public services, Modern management and e-government are two central means of achieving fundamental changes in public administration. The goal is an administration that does more and costs less. E-government projects are not only modernizing public agencies and authorities, but also making administrative procedures more transparent for ordinary citizens, which in turn also makes new demands on personnel to be more accountable.

Managers must respond flexibly to the changing demands and expectations of the public and the ever changing nature of public problems, yet they must do so in a manner that provides accountability to the public and political overseers. A dichotomous approach to the study of leadership as management action and the governance structures within which managers operate has inhibited the search for a public management theory that reconciles the dilemma. Managers must attend to demands for both flexible leadership action and structures that promise accountability. The capacity to perceive this relationship offers managers a means to keep flexibility and accountability in a dynamic tension. It has been suggested that public management scholars can elevate this understanding form an implicit "theory in use" to an explicit "espoused theory". This approach could be a productive one for public management scholarship and. ultimately for its practice. (Feldman and Khademian, 2001, 339-61).

(vi) Combating Corruption for Good Governance

From the foregoing discussion, it is more than evident that the concept of quality governance is premised on a corruption free administrative system. Combating corruption for sustainable development calls for : (a) reducing opportunities and incentives for corrupt behaviour and increasing the sense of accountability on the part of public officials, and (b) effective implementation of anti-corruption measures, which would imply that measures should be logically consistent with regard to the phasing of a time table for speedy investigation and conviction; a strong political commitment to implement the strategies and enforcing anti-corruption measures; and people's active participation from below in the enforcement of administrative, legal and judicial measures, thus mobilizing the public against corruption in public life.

Apart from the above fundamental conditions, it must be emphasized that fighting corruption requires: (a) formation of a national coordinating body that should be responsible for devising and following up on a strategy against corruption, along with a citizen's oversight board; (b) the existence of a high powered independent prosecuting body to investigate and prosecute all such known cases of corruption; (c) and the setting up of special courts for trying such cases at a stretch so that the cases come to their legitimate conclusion without any delay; (d) thoroughly overhauling and reforming the system of electoral laws and economic regulations minimizing the temptation to indulge in corruption practice; (e) enactment of an appropriate legislation to limit the number of Ministries and Departments both at the Centre and the states so that the temptation of expanding ministries only for political gains could be minimized; and (e) by providing specialized technical assistance to anti-corruption agencies organizing high-level anti-corruption workshops or strategic consulting or hiring international investigations to track down ill-gotten deposits overseas.

At the same time, it is also important that international institutions should take steps to encourage participatory approaches in developing countries in order to build consensus for anti-corruption drives and associated reforms. Civil society is likely to be a major ally in resisting corruption. More and more it is this ally that seeks concrete support from more developed Western countries and international agencies in actively combating corruption (Kaufman, 1997, 130). International cooperation can help national leaders develop political resolve, and international action can convey the useful truth that we are all involved in the problem of corruption and that we must find solutions together.

VI

REINVENTING GOOD GOVERNANCE FOR SUSTAINABLE DEVELOPMENT IN INDIA

In order to meet the challenges of good governance for promoting human security, a six pronged strategy needs to be adopted at this juncture of the evolution of the Indian Polity: which may as well be relevant for other developing societies.

(a) On the institutional front, it is necessary to regenerate political and administrative institutions from the virtual collapse that India has experienced in the last four decades—restore the legitimacy and effectiveness of the legislature, bureaucracy, the judiciary and the non-state actors of the civil society. As the 'sustainability of transition' in India has been greatly affected by the gradual incremental loss of the capacity and effectiveness of the democratic institutions, it is necessary that a radical package of reforms to revamp the institutional framework be implemented immediately. At the same time, it is necessary to consolidate and operationalize the gains of decentralization of authority and empowerment of the people especially the weaker and vulnerable sections of the population in reality, affected by the 73rd and 74th Amendments of the Constitution. Initiatives for local planning coupled with augmenting of local resources is of utmost for restoring the credibility of sub-national and local institutions.

(b) In respect of the administrative system, there is an immediate need to cut down the size of the government and its expenditure. As a former Indian Minister of Finance, Mr. Yashwant Sinha has once so categorically stated that while external borrowings are being used for productive purposes, the internal borrowings were going towards meeting establishment costs. It is necessary to reverse the trend as early as possible.

(c) One of the other measures adopted in many western countries to ensure transparency in the functioning of the government and to fight corruption and mal-administration is the enactment of Public Interest Disclosure Acts popularly called Whistle-blower Acts. The object of such elements is to improve accountability in government and public sector organizations by encouraging people not to turn a blind eye to mal-practice taking place in their organizations and to report the same to the appropriate authority in a confidential manner or by a public report. Although the Government of India has not been able to enact such an Act, but it has lately been quite concerned to protect the identity and person of such officials, albeit with little success, who have dared to come out openly to disclose administrative malpractices to the public. There is a need for the enactment of such a law to encourage persons to come out openly when they smell of scams or corruption in the government.

(d) Transparency in administrative procedures and decision-making is an important ingredient of 'good governance'. Although the Government of India has enacted the Right to Information Act, 2005 as one of the steps towards that goal, but its implementation in the last few years has raised a lot of controversy and confusion, which need to be clarified immediately for its smooth operation (Jain, 2006).

(e) Simultaneously the bureaucracy is to be revamped in terms of change in its orientation, behaviour and attitude. In stead of being the defender of the *status quo*, there has to be a realisation that with the advent of globalisation, liberalisation and privatisation, it has to play a major role of a catalyst for change. Apart from the changes in the traditional values and norms of work culture, it has to demonstrate its willingness to accept new technical innovations and values of achievement and competition, equity and egalitarianism and concern for broader collective social goals.

Besides absorbing the values of participatory democracy, decentralization of authority and power, bureaucracy has not only to observe a modicum of transparency and concede an appropriate right of information to the people in its decision-making process, but has also to secure a balance between a rule-bound administration and an administration that can effectively and quickly deliver results, particularly in developmental and social welfare activities.

The bureaucracy is also both under legal and moral obligation to exercise its authority and discretionary powers with a view to meet the norms of responsiveness and accountability. Apart from its professional norms of efficiency, effectiveness, economy and cost consciousness, the core public service values of integrity, impartiality and responsibility need to be observed if the gains of the process of liberalisation are to be consolidated for protecting human security.

(f) On the economic front, it is of utmost importance that a comprehensive and concerted policy strategy based on general consensus be developed for : (i) revamping public distribution system (PDS), (ii) disinvestment in public enterprises in key economic sectors like power, energy, oil, transport, telecommunication and in sick industrial units, (iii) reconsideration of proportion of subsidies in agricultural, oil, and other key sectors of the economy, which are at best counter-productive, and (iv) creating public-private synergy in collaborative governance, and adopting a viable pattern of contracting out and outsourcing of delivery of public services at the local levels of governance with appropriate safeguards for accountability, standards of services and redressal of public complaints.

(g) In respect of social security, the system of governance faces a massive challenge to provide for adequate employment generation, good health, universal education system, shelter, and the basic facilities of sanitation and drinking water. Providing for higher outlays and spending on items like primary education and primary health-care is not the solution alone, the real challenge is effective management on the part of the administration to deliver these goods at the lowest costs and in an equitable manner. These are some of the areas where the state cannot abdicate its responsibilities notwithstanding the emphasis of liberalization and privatization, increased public and foreign investments, and contracting out of the services in various industrial and other sectors of the economy and social services, and finally,

(h) Utilizing the tools of technology and "on-line governance", wherever feasible, for quick delivery of services providing information and redressal of grievances. In the management of public services, the adoption of information technology is essential to the efficiency of public administration. Communication to the public through the Internet and other media is required to achieve transparency—a condition for accountability.

Concluding Observations

In conclusion, however, it should be remembered that for achieving good governance, no amount of planning and thinking in all these areas would be useful unless the governments at all levels of the polity are capable enough to take hard and unpleasant decisions and have the will and capacity to implement and continuously monitor and evaluate their impact. At the same time, the political leadership has to demonstrate its strong determination to undertake reforms by first cleaning its own stable from corrupt and criminal influences, and setting ethical standards of quality governance both at the political and administrative levels. For changes to come, it is necessary to change the mindset and attitudes of both the public administrators and the politicians in power (Mathur, 343).

In the perspectives of the worldwide developments at the threshold of the 21st century, we have attempted at discussing some of the emerging challenges to quality and "good governance", on which the strategies for growth and sustainable development in India and in other transitional societies can be built and operationalized. It is heartening that people in almost all developing countries have recognized their importance, and it is likely that the growing concerns towards SD, fighting corruption and devising innovations for "quality governance" may turn out to be a concerted international movement, not confined merely to the realm of academic discussions or writings in specific contexts like India, but of taking constructive actions for positive results transcending the jurisdictions of national boundaries. This is the only hope for achieving a universally good, and corruption-free good governance, for the very survival of humanity, towards which we must all strive.

References

Approach Paper to the Tenth Five Year Plan (2002-07), (New Delhi, Planning Commission, 2001), para 1.9, p. 2, and 49.

Brinkerhoff, Derick W., and Jennifer M. Coston (1999) "International Development Management in a Globalized World" in *Public Administration Review*, July/August 1999, Vol. 59, No. 4., pp. 346-61.

Considine, Mark (2002), "The End of the Line? Accountable Governance in the age of Networks, Partnerships, and Joined-up Services:" in *Governance: An International Journal of Policy, Administration, and Institutions*, Vol. 15, No. 1 (January 2002) pp. 21-40.

Dwivedi, O.P. (1987), "Moral Dimensions of Statecraft", *Canadian Journal of Political Science*, Vol. 20, No. 4 (1987), pp. 609-709 And "The Challenge of Cultural Diversity for Good Governance", a paper prepared for presentation at the UN meeting on Managing Diversity in the Civil Service, organized by the UN Division of Public Economics and Public Administration (DPEPA), UN Department of Economic and Social Affairs, New York, NY, USA, 3-4 May 2001.

Feldman, Martha S., and Anne M. Khademian (2001) "Principles for Public Management Practice: From Dichotomies to Interdependence" in *Governance: An International Journal of Policy and Administration*, Vol. 14, No. 3, July 2001, pp. 339-61.

Fuhr, Harald (2003), "Constructive Pressures and Incentives to Reform: Globalization and its Impact on Public Sector Performance and Governance in Developing Countries", a paper prepared for presentation in Panel RC 4.2 at the 19th Congress of the International Political Science Association, held at Durban (S. Africa), June-July 2003.

Government of India (2000), *Economic Survey, 1999-2000*, New Delhi, Government of India, Ministry of Finance, 2000, p. 164.

India Today, 11 December 2000, pp. 70-76.

Jain, R.B. (1989), *Bureaucratic Politics in the Third World*, (New Delhi, Gitanjali Publishing House, 1989), pp. 362-74.

Jain, R.B. (2001), *Public Administration in India: 21st Century Challenges to Good Governance*, (New Delhi, Deep & Deep, 2001.

———, (2006), "Opening Government for Public Scrutiny: An Analysis of Recent Efforts in India to make Governance more Transparent and Accountable" in *Indian Journal of Public Administration*, Vol. 52, No. 3 (July September 2006), See pp. 555-60 for a detailed discussion and analysis of the enactment and implementation of the Right to Information Act, 2005.

———, (2007), 'Revamping the Administrative Structure and Processes in India for Online Democracy" in Ari-Veikko Anttiroiko and Matti Malkia (ed.) *Encyclopedia of Digital Government*, Finland, Vol. III (I-Z) (2007), pp. 1418-23.

Kaufman, Daniel (1997), "Corruption: The Facts", *Foreign Policy*, Summer 1997, p. 130.

Kaufman, Daniel (2001), "New Empirical Frontiers in Fighting Corruption and Improving Governance—Selected Issues", a paper presented at the OSCE Economic Forum, Brussels, January 30, 31, 2001, p. 6.

Knill, Christoph and Dirk Lehmkuhl (2002), "Private Actors and the State: Internationalization and Changing Patterns of Governance" in *Governance: An International Journal of Policy, Administration and Institutions* (Oxford), Vol. 15, No. 1 (January 2002), pp. 41-63.

Luo Xiao-hua has in an Electronic Contribution has Subscribed to this fact see: http://doi.ieeecomputersociety.org/10.1109/ICMeCG.2009.96

Mathur, B.P. (2005), *Governance Reform for Vision India* (New Delhi, Macmillan, 2005), p. 343.

Parr, Saikko Fuuda (1997), *Sustainable Human Development in a Globalizing World* (New York, Human Development Report Office, 1997), pp. 1-2.

Singh, Tavleen (2000), "Poverty Politics" in *India Today*, 11 December 2000, p. 26.

Stuijvenberg, Peter A. Van (1996), "Structural Adjustment in India—What About Poverty Alleviation?", in Hanumantha Rao, C.H. and Hans Linnemann (eds.), *Economic Reforms and Poverty Alleviation in India* (New Delhi: Sage Publications, 1996), pp. 31-89.

Towards Faster and more Inclusive Growth: *An Approach to the XIth Five Year Plan (2007-12)*, Government of India, Planning Commission, New Delhi, December 2007.

Globalization, NPM and Good Governance

INTRODUCTION

The decade of 1990s has been a decade of exceptional changes in the theory and practice of good governance. The changes in question have increasingly been treated under the rubric of "globalization", a catch all phrase which emphasizes the emergence of a truly global economy and a shift towards "world capitalism", signifying a movement toward a new era of both vastly more powerful and essentially different corporate forms and processes, which has in all societies affected the existing forms of governance and citizen identity. Three important movements that have made important strides during this decade in meeting the challenges of this transformation have been Reinventing Government, the New Public Management (NPM) and a call for the Downsizing of Public Bureaucracies.

Public Administration in India as elsewhere has not completely remained untouched by these global developments and has in various ways attempted to incorporate some of the precepts drawn from these movements. To what extent the administrative system in India has been successful in its efforts to modernise itself, and utilise the lessons emanating from the experiences of other administrative systems undergoing transformation under the spell of one or the other of the above movements is a question which cannot be answered in one way or the other. However, it would be helpful to review what particular steps have been adopted in India for achieving some positive goals of these alternative precepts in public management and to analyze the emerging ethical concerns as a consequence thereof.

I

POLICY OF GLOBALIZATION AND LIBERALIZATION IN INDIA : THE BACKGROUND

After attaining Independence in 1947, India embarked on the experiment to constitute itself into a sovereign republic and modernize the state and its administration through the adoption of a 'parliamentary democracy'. At that time not many scholars and analysts in the world had believed that India will survive as a democratic nation negating John Stuart Mill's contention that 'democracy' is "next to impossible: in multi-ethnic societies and completely 'impossible in linguistically divided countries'," as well as Robert Delhi's belief "that widespread poverty and illiteracy are anaethema to 'stable democracy'—a concept that is supposedly linked with the level of socio-economic development". [Lijphart, 1996: 258-268] However, these early foreboding and later predictions that "the odds are almost wholly against the survival of freedom and . . . the issue is, in fact, whether any Indian state can survive at all" [Harrison, 1960: 338] have been proved wrong. India's existence as a democratic state since the last 63 years of its Independence has compelled scholars to evolve a new consociational interpretation of the survival of democracy in deeply divided societies. [Lijphart, 1996]

Over all these years, while evolving a consensual framework of a democratic government, the leadership in India has also from time to time attempted to devise strategies for good governance, which is associated with an efficient and effective development-oriented, citizen-friendly and responsive administration committed to improvement in quality of life of the people.

The Government of India has adopted policies of globalization, liberalisation and market economy in the wake of the serious economic crisis that enveloped the country by the middle of 1991. The crisis arose due to the economic consequences of upheavals in the erstwhile USSR and East Europe—the effects of the Gulf War, the shifts in the global economic power balance and the economic policies followed by the Union and the State Governments since the 1930s. The immediate reason was a serious balance of payments crisis owing to a steady decline in exports, negative growth rates in industry and agriculture, and 0.3 per cent decline in the domestic production of crude oil. Among the long-term domestic factors contributing to high cost and low productivity were: (a) the inadequate returns and continuing losses from the massive investments in the public sector undertakings; and (b) economic populism resulting in increasing state subsidies, especially in fertilizers and writing-off loans to farmers and hidden payments incurred through lower tariff rates of state undertakings in power and transport sectors.

India's adoption of a programme of globalization market economy and competitiveness came after more than 6 months of negotiations with the World Bank starting in January 1991. The package of reform measures announced by the then newly installed Narasimha Rao Government in July 1991 consisted of two separate economic policies: (a) a macro-economic stabilization programme (IMF inspired) essentially focusing on reducing the twin deficits on the balance of payment and on the state budget; and (b) a comprehensive programme for structural change of the economy (World Bank inspired) in the fields of trade, industry, foreign investments, public sector and the financial sector among others. [For a comprehensive discussion on this topic, See Jain and Bongartz, 1994.]

'Globalization', 'competitiveness' and 'liberalisation' come to India as a booster, and through the backdoor of "economic reforms". The sanctity of economic reforms had been derived from it. It was argued that progress is taking place though globalization, and economic reforms are the only means to join in this process. Hence economic reforms are the only alternative for human security and India's future. Globalization as a phenomenon involves two different entities : (a) finance capital through multi-national corporations, and (b) new technologies such as computers and telecommunications. It was argued that the growth and internationalization of finance capital is good and desirable for projects because it promotes growth of technology. Globalization provides a useful means to develop technologies necessary for the production of goods and services that improve our well-being.

The post-1991 economic reforms were initially launched under compelling balance of payments crisis. At the same time it was felt that by adopting market-oriented and globally competitive restructuring policies somewhat similar to those of Southeast Asian countries, the Indian economy could grow much faster and become more self-reliant in managing its balance of payments and could at the same time speedily accelerate growth and reduce the level of poverty, thus contributing to human security including freedom from hunger, disease, ignorance, unemployment and homelessness.

II

THE NEW PUBLIC MANAGEMENT (NPM) PARADIGM AND GOVERNANCE IN INDIA

In the early 1990s, a new managerial approach to public administration, known as the new public management (NPM), began to take hold in the United States and other industrialized countries [Hood, 1991; Osborne and Gaebler, 1992; Gore, 1993; Mascarenhas, 1993; Masser, 1998]. The globalization of public administration spread the concept of NPM and its attendant reforms in the developing countries as well. Applications of NPM in the developing countries has also been supported and reinforced by international aid funding agencies. The new approach is reform-oriented and seeks to improve public sector performance. It starts from the premise that traditional bureaucratically organized public administration has become dysfunctional and consequently the public has lost faith in government. After years of anti-government political rhetoric, bureaucrat bashing, and negative press coverage, public administration was broadly viewed as inept and wasteful, needing drastic reforms, even reinvention [Osborne and Gaebler, 1992]. The NPM represents a major shift in paradigm from traditional public administration. It focuses attention on the achievement of results and the personal responsibility of managers. Similarly, it requires additional emphasis on program evaluation, performance measurements, and increased importation of private sector practices into the area of public management. Advocates of NPM argue that by enhancing the elements of accountability, responsibility, free flow of information, and streamlined management, public management has the potential to contribute to the establishment of good governance [Barzelay, 2001; Barberis, 1998; Ferlie *et. al.*, 1996, Soni (2007), pp. 84-95]

Taken as a whole the NPM and reinventing government reforms embrace the following premises: (1) public administration should focus on achieving results rather than primarily conforming to the processes, (2) it should make better use of market like competition in the provision of goods and services to achieve results, (3) the agencies should view the public and their clients as customers to whom they should be responsive, (4) government should consider privatization and contracting out production and delivery of services where possible, (5) government agencies should be deregulated implying that the traditional emphasis on centralized control of staffing, budgeting, and procurement is inappropriate for a results-oriented government, (6) agencies should empower employees to use their creativity in serving customers and doing their jobs, and (7) public administration culture should change to be flexible, innovative, problem-solving, entrepreneurial, as opposed to rule-bound, process-oriented, and focused on inputs rather than results [Borins, 1998].

Bardouille (2000) argues that globalization has been the principle catalyst for the proliferation of NPM concepts and practices. The NPM enables new framework of governance to be employed by the state so as to manage its changing role in a globalizing world. It is no coincidence that NPM-related instruments and principles have rapidly gained currency in the past two decades in the same period in which dramatic systemic changes have taken place in the international economy. These changes are consistent with the state's efforts to respond to the pressures of globalization. This effort by the state to respond to the imperative of globalization involves fostering and formalizing a more competitive and entrepreneurial spirit in the state functions. Efficiency is increasingly becoming the primary determinant of how viable a state can be in a world where state boundaries are being liberalized at an unprecedented rate. [Soni 2007, in Jain (2007), pp. 84-85]

It can thus be argued that the NPM paradigm provides for a caring government that is transparent, focused on the people and characterized by commitment, accountability, responsiveness and inclusiveness [Kim (2005), pp. 1-32 and 95-152. Also see Reddy (2006) pp. 566-91] It has had far-reaching impact on reshaping public administrative systems in both the developed and developing countries and meeting the challenges posed by 'globalization'. [Jain (ed.), (2007), pp. 67-68]

Introducing NPM in the Governance of India

During the late 1990s, under the impact of these developments, the Government of India felt the need to restructure and reorient the administrative system and to adopt a normative model of *Good Management Approach* towards public administration. This was to include : (a) A more strategic or result-oriented (efficiency, effectiveness and service quality) orientation to decision-making; (b) Replacement of highly centralised organizational structures with decentralised management environment integrating with the new Panchayati Raj and Municipal Institutions, where decisions on resource allocation and service delivery are taken close to the point of delivery; (c) Flexibility to explore alternatives to direct public provision which might provide more cost effective policy outcomes; (d) Focusing attention on the matching of authority and responsibility as a key to improving performance, including mechanism of explicit performance contracting; (e) Creating of competitive environments within and between public service organisations; (f) Strengthening of strategic capacities at the Center to steer government to respond to external changes and diverse interests quickly, flexibly and at least costs; (g) Greater accountability and transparency through requirements to report on results and their full costs; (h) Service wide budgeting and management systems to support and encourage these changes; (i) Breaking the growing nexus of bureaucrats, politicians and criminals to restore public confidence in public management system amongst the citizenry; (j) Adapting of innovations and evolving suitable mechanism to eliminate corruption at both political and administrative levels and strengthen citizens' grievance redressal system; (k) Downsizing of bureaucracy and improving the system of delivery at the cutting edge of administration by replacing the existing archaic bureaucratic procedures by absorbing some appropriate precepts inherent in the philosophy of New Public Management; (l) Effectively utilising the fruits of technical revolution and the Information Management system for an effective and quick public service delivery system; and (m) Making improvements in the working atmosphere of the government institutions and offices to reflect a new work culture and a changed administrative behaviour incorporating the principles of transparency, responsiveness, accountability, participative and citizen-friendly management.

Simultaneously the bureaucracy was to be revamped in terms of change in its orientation, behaviour and attitude. Instead of being the defender of the *status quo*, there has to be a realization that with the advent of globalization, liberalization and privatization, it has to play a major role of a catalyst for change. Apart from the changes in the traditional values and norms of work culture, it has to demonstrate its willingness to accept new technical innovations and values of achievement and competition, equity and egalitarianism and concern for broader collective social goals.

Despite certain steps in administrative reforms for good governance triggered by the Government of India Ministers meetings in 1997, and a concerted movement towards E-governance, the reform efforts in terms of reorienting the behaviour of public servants towards public welfare and introducing ethics in administration did not achieve much success. The Second Administrative Reforms Commission constituted in 2005 under the chairmanship of Veerappa Moily is now looking into this crucial aspect of introducing ethics in public administration. Before analyzing the Moily Commission's recommendations in this respect, it will be of interest to briefly discuss the some emerging ethical dilemmas of public governance in post-NPM and globalization era.

III

THE NPM AND THE EMERGING MORAL DILEMMAS

As many scholars have perceived, the adoption of the NPM strategy for revamping public administration changes the focus of attention on 'citizenry', which brings inevitable tensions, e.g. between providing a quality service to the citizen or providing an economical, low cost service to the State. The post-NPM developments in Public Administration and governance derive from the adoption and evolution of *managerialism* central notions. In fact, downsizings, privatisations, public-private partnerships, and restructurings are modern phenomena that raise countless and complex ethical doubts. [Bilhim and Neves, 2005), p. 10] Effectively, if normative foundations for public administration are still ambiguous and non-defined, particularly in developing democracies, how can we identify norms for the context of frequent developments in a changing public administration? Which are the consequences of these new formats in administration terms, of clarification of responsibilities, of managers' action and their orientation? How is their effective relationship with the citizens? In addition, what about their statute while users? Are they considered citizens or customers? Who can be held responsible for errors made by computers and technologies? Besides these necessary reflections and answers, we live in an era, when a crisis of values appears to be evident. [*Ibid.*] The Governance has to face continuously great expectations of citizens, combined with the evaluation criteria of efficiency, effectiveness, economy and value. In fact, the economic conception of public service leads us to the idea of delivering a good or a service below its cost, not forgetting quality and the essential factors named above. [*Ibid.*]

Because of the wholesale adoption of the NPM paradigm, market-driven management views in the public sector have emerged as an all encompassing approach in the practice of public management. Proponents of this neo-managerialism expect that it would turn public managers into risk-taking entrepreneurial leaders rather than being merely instrument of public policy. These leaders are expected to function in an environment that is empowering, catalytic, mission and customer driven, results-oriented, and market-oriented, i.e., leveraging change through the market [Osborne and Gaebler, 1992]. The problem with this model, argue the opponents, is that these ideas are difficult to reconcile with democratic accountability requiring public managers to be in the service of the public interest. The manager is no longer a servant of the people, as integrity, truthfulness equity and fairness become significantly undermined in the pursuit of the bottom line. NPM also emphasizes the strategic management and performance measurement. However, critics argue that these measurements are often directed at short-run results which fail to provide any meaningful assessment of the success of longer-term policy mandates of the state [Haque, 1996a; Bowornwathana, 2001]. Supporters, on the other hand, claim that the NPM has promoted innovation and radical change in the public service, and therefore, it is worth pursuing even though democratic accountability and the entrepreneurial-bureaucrat might be hard to reconcile.

Scholars, however, caution that although the NPM paradigm appears attractive, care must be exercised in applying it in developing countries. [Haque, 1996a; Bowornwathana, 2001]. Cheung [1997] also argues against the importation of most fashionable Western paradigms and recommends the reconnecting of the domestic society to governance. Many of the prerequisites of new public management are related to the level of development of a country, e.g., the maturity of its political system and the capacity of the economy to finance the experiment. The cultural aspects also must be taken into consideration. In societies where the public sector has traditionally played a dominant role in service provision and where the public do not have the financial capability to obtain goods and services in a competitive market, the NPM model may not work.

In their study of Public Administration in Portugal, referred to above, Bilhim and Neves [Bilhim and Neves, 2005, pp. 10-13] identify a number of factors which justify the magnitude of the ethics in a contemporary public administration, more concretely:

- material and resource difficulties,
- needs of a growing and multifaceted society,
- critical and attentive perspective implied in citizenship,
- restructuring subjects and change of the administration, and
- constant demand that decision processes become more thoroughly participated.

The ethics of this new millennium concerns employee and service, so it involves the absolute need of an orientation according to clear and internalized values, especially for the higher administration levels. It is crucial to have a leadership that provides the integration of these values; a strong organizational culture based on those principles, a serious evaluation/attendance and an Aristotelian process of learning and continuous recycling. This accomplishment lives in a real political will for true ethical politics, homogeneous and global. It is essential to pass from impositions of bureaucratic sense to internalized practices, consensual conducts, conception of systems and organizational structures.

In effect, the present reality requires innovative approaches and combined measures. For that reason, Bilhim and Neves suggest that a public administration ethics framing can be consummate with the following joint procedures:

- Accountability Tools,
- Conduct Codes,
- Monitoring Mechanisms (e.g. internal and external questionnaires),
- Development of Supportive Structures (to encourage ethical conduct and to reward those who act morally),
- Implementation of Audit Methods at Inter-governmental level,

- Professional Socialization (e.g. formation, awareness and training),
- Introduction of whistle-blowing systems (in a careful way),
- A stronger appeal to the active participation of citizens (for instance in the denunciation of bad practices),
- Definition of Leadership Responsibilities, and
- Assertive Communication. [*Ibid.*, pp. 13-14]

In the background of above analysis, it will be interesting to examine to what extent and with what strategies Public Administration in India has responded to the above approaches and strategies to weave the various ethical concerns raised above.

IV

GLOBALIZATION, NPM AND THE ETHICAL CHALLENGES IN INDIA

As noted above, the developing countries have to tread with extreme caution in initiating changes in public management, particularly in anticipation of the potential conflict between firmly entrenched values and practices and new ideas and innovations. The Indian experience of ten years of globalization and competitiveness clearly indicates that even as its GDP is growing at a considerable pace than earlier, and there is unexpected dynamism on the industrial front, the negative fall out of rampant consumerism and individualism has made a dent on the old community and kin networks. The quality of life in terms of environment and aesthetics is deteriorating and the criminalisation and lumpenisation of polity and society is rising at a frightening rate, leading to a call on the part of many thinkers for alternative development paradigm. Thus it has been argued that if the erosion of cultural, family and community values as well as environment and natured resources is to stop, if an inner bearing, a sense of well being and identity are not to be lost in the process of development, then culture and cultural values must be seen as determining of the process and not merely its consequence.

These have to be integrated accordingly into policy processes, project design and funding by government, private and international agencies alike should form a part of the ongoing process of globalization, liberalization and competitiveness.

Probity in Governance

The basic ethical issue in the post-Globalizaion-NPM era has thus been to ensure probity in governance. The important requisite for ensuring probity in governance is absence of corruption, effective laws, rules, and regulations governing every aspect of public life and, more important, an effective and fair implementation of those laws. The National Commission on the Review of the Working of the Constitution (NCRWC) has explored whether some legislative measures can be designed to ensure probity in governance, although it felt that instilling a sense of discipline among the citizens and the public services is more the function of the society, its leaders, political parties and public figures and less a matter which can be legislated upon. However, while endorsing the recommendations of the Nolan Committee in UK discussed below, it felt that some legislative measures: like enacting a Whistle Blowing Act, Enactment of a Freedom of Information Act, necessity of a Lok Pal (Ombudsman) Act, Vigilance Commission Act, establishment of a Civil Service Commission Board, Strengthening of Criminal Justice System, and the enactment of a Public Service Ethics Act on the lines of Ethics in Government Act of USA were absolutely necessary, and recommended their enactment. [See NCRWC, 2002; Kashyap (ed.), 2006, pp. 232-52.]

Ethical Behaviour of Public Services

This brings us to another core issue of promoting ethical behaviour of public administrators. As stated earlier, the Nolan Committee in the U.K. in mid-nineties had emphasized the seven principles of public life: (a) *Selflessness:* Holders of public office should act solely in terms of the public interest. They should not do so in order to gain financial or other material benefits for themselves, their family, or their friends, (b) *Integrity:* Holders of public office should not place themselves under any financial or other obligations to outside individuals or organizations that might seek to influence them in the performance of their official duties, (c) *Objectivity:* In carrying out public business, including making public appointments, awarding contracts or recommending individuals for rewards and benefits, holders of public office should make choices on merit, (d) *Accountability*: Holders of public office are accountable for their decisions and actions to the public and must submit themselves to whatever scrutiny is appropriate to their office, (e) *Openness*: Holders of public office should be as open as possible about all the decisions and actions to the public and must submit themselves to whatever scrutiny is appropriate to their office, (f) *Honesty:* Holders of public office have a duty to declare any private interests relating to their public duties and to take steps to resolve any conflicts arising in a way that protects the public interest, and (g) *Leadership*: Holders of public office should promote and support these principles by leadership and example. The observation of these principles by public administrators in the perspective of Globalization and NPM is indeed a big step in the promotion of public ethics. [Nolan Report (1995): Report on Standards in Public Life, www.archive.official-documents.co.uk/documetns/parliament]

At the same time, bureaucracy is also both under legal and moral obligation to exercise its authority and discretionary powers with a view to meet the norms of responsiveness and accountability. Apart from its professional norms of efficiency, effectiveness, economy and cost consciousness, the core public service values of integrity, impartiality and responsibility need to be observed if the gains of the process of liberalization are to be consolidated for protecting human security.

Ethical Standards in the Existing Conduct Rules for Public Services in India

There is no Code of Ethics prescribed for civil servants in India although such codes exist in other countries. What we have in India are several Conduct Rules, which prohibit a set of common activities.

These Conduct Rules do serve a purpose, but they do not constitute a Code of Ethics. In the 1930s, a compendium of instructions containing 'do's and don'ts was issued and collectively called 'Conduct Rules'. The compendium was converted in the form of distinct rules in 1955. The Santhanam Committee on Prevention of Corruption recommended considerable enlargement of such rules resulting in the 1964 version. These rules have subsequently been updated to include additional norms of behaviour. Some of the additions are :

- the requirement of observing courtesy,
- prohibiting demanding and accepting dowry,
- prohibiting sexual harassment of women employees, and, recently,
- prohibition to employ children below 14 years of age as domestic help.

The code of behaviour as enunciated in the Conduct Rules, while containing some general norms like 'maintaining integrity and absolute devotion to duty' and not indulging in 'conduct unbecoming of a government servant', is generally directed towards cataloguing specific activities deemed undesirable for government servants. [Second Administrative Reforms Commission, 2007, pp. 44ff]

Forms of Unethical Conduct

It will be fruitful to analyze as to what constitute an unethical conduct on the part of public servants: Ethical problems and concerns often are the result of social influences on public servants. The most important of such influences result from the activities of elected representatives, party officials, and other politicians. Examples are:

- influence-peddling and acting as a broker between a business concern and government; politicising the interpretation and enforcement of laws and decrees;
- censoring or muzzling the mass media so that anti-regime views are not published;
- appointing political supporter; and defeated party candidates to government boards and commissions;
- interfering in normal personnel practices to secure public service appointments and promotions for supporters and sympathisers;

- the direct or indirect sale of public offices, government contracts, monopolies, licences, and loans;
- the improper use of police and military forces in the normal functioning of community affairs;
- manipulation in the purchase of machinery, property, equipment and services for government departments;
- misuse of official and confidential information for private gain; and
- the concentration of extra-legal authority (and the use of it) in the hands of few persons.

These activities, when supported by social values which judge everything in terms of money, along with the emergence of new economically powerful classes which seek immediate gain by using political power and social prestige, become powerful factors in determining the environment to which employees must adjust. Ethical confusion and moral dilemmas will abound. [Dwivedi and Jain, 1985, Chs. VI and VII]. It must, however, be noted that that these patterns of unethical conduct can easily lead to administrative and bureaucratic corruption. In fact it is very difficult to say when an unethical conduct becomes a corrupt practice. The line of distinction between the two is very thin.

Curbing Conflict of Interests of Public Services

There is, of late, a concern that more 'generic norms' need to be added to the list of accepted conduct. In this context, conflict of interest is an important area which should be adequately addressed in these codes. It is necessary to build safeguards to prevent conflict of interest.

A draft 'Public Service Bill' now under consideration of the Ministry of Personnel, Public Grievances and Pensions seeks to lay down a number of generic expectations from civil servants, which are referred to as "values". The salient 'values' envisaged in the Bill are:

- Allegiance to the various ideals enshrined in the preamble to the Constitution.
- Apolitical functioning.

- Good governance for betterment of the people to be the primary goal of civil service.
- Duty to act objectively and impartially.
- Accountability and transparency in decision-making.
- Maintenance of highest ethical standards.
- Merit to be the criteria in selection of civil servants consistent, however, with the cultural, ethnic and other diversities of the nation.
- Ensuring economy and avoidance of wastage in expenditure.
- Provision of healthy and congenial work environment.
- Communication, consultation and cooperation in performance of functions, i.e. participation of all levels of personnel in management.

The Draft Bill also Envisages a Public Service Code and a Public Service Management

Code laying down more specific duties and responsibilities. Violation of the Code would invite punishments akin to the current major and minor penalties by the heads of institutions/organizations. A 'Public Service Authority ' is also envisaged to oversee implementation of the Code and values indicated above and to render advice in the matter of the values and the Code. The Commission has decided that a detailed examination of the proposed draft Bill will be appropriately made in its forthcoming report on Civil Services Reforms. [Second Administrative Reforms Commission, 2007, pp. 9-11 and 44-48, accessed from *www.arc.gov.nic.in*]

The various issues discussed above are not significant only for the civil services. They are important for all segments of the bureaucracy and, equally so, for all local bodies and their employees.

Promoting Ethics in Outsourced and Contractual Services as a Sequel to NPM

One of the emerging key issues as a sequel to the impact of NPM in Public Administration is the issue of promoting ethical behaviour not only amongst public services directly under the government, but also of those responsible for delivery of public services in areas of outsourcing operations as a result of public-private cooperation, who are outside the direct control of the government. It is not only an issue of imbibing ethical values of service and responsiveness among all the public employees, but also of improving the administrative environment in which they work and live For this it is necessary (a) that codes and/or Laws on Ethical Standards and anti-corruption, etc. be made public; (b) institutional changes and reforms to create an ethical framework be continued; (c) audit, agencies be strengthened for accountability, and openness; (d) guiding principles and motivation should be encouraged through leadership/example and appropriate personnel procedures; and (e) culture and values of the society be identified as important and reflected in the codes/laws/ principles/education/training and in ethical policies made by government(s) as well as business corporations for a fair, objective and compassionate society. [Jain, R.B. (2000)]

Managing Public Ethics in India

As has been pointed out above, the Portugese study by Bilhim and Neves has outlined some new ethical challenges as a result of the impact of Globalization and the NPM movement. They suggest that a public administration ethics framing can be consummate with the following joint procedures: [Bilhim and Neves, 2005, pp. 13-14]

- Accountability Tools,
- Conduct Codes,
- Monitoring Mechanisms (e.g. internal and external questionnaires),
- Development of Supportive Structures (to encourage ethical conduct and to reward those who act morally),
- Implementation of Audit Methods at Inter-governmental level,
- Professional Socialization (e.g. formation, awareness and training),
- Introduction of whistle-blowing systems (in a careful way),
- A stronger appeal to the active participation of citizens (for instance in the denunciation of bad practices),
- Definition of Leadership Responsibilities, and
- Assertive Communication [*Ibid.*].

The Government of India is now beset with a number of new ethical challenges arising out of the impact of globalization. Besides absorbing the values of participatory democracy, decentralization of authority and power, bureaucracy in India has not only to observe a modicum of transparency and concede an appropriate right of information to the people in its decision-making process, (which has recently been attempted through the enactment of Right to Information Act in 2005), but has also to secure a balance between a rule-bound administration and an administration that can effectively and quickly deliver results, particularly in developmental and social welfare activities.

In order to combat the total lack of a notion of accountability and responsiveness on the part of government functionaries both legislators and administrators, which has eroded the very essence of a responsible government, the Government of India had in 1996 devised an "Action Plan for an Effective and Responsive Administration". The Action Plan included initiatives in four specific areas:

> (a) Making Administration Accountable and Citizen-friendly, (b) Ensuring Transparency by introducing the Right to Information, (c) Taking measures to cleanse and motivate Public Services, and (d) Introduction of E-Governance for greater openness, reduction of red-tape and quick and convenient interaction of citizens with the government. [Jain (2004), pp. 31-33.]

Realizing that the secrecy and the lack of openness in official transactions, a colonial legacy which somehow persisted all through the five decades of India's Independence, was responsible for corruption in administration, apart from being contrary to the spirit of an accountable and democratic Government, the Government of India addressed itself to the problem of ensuring freedom of information to the public and to amend such laws that stipulate necessary access of the public to information. As a result, a number of statutory schemes were formulated to amend various existing central and state legislations in order to improve the access of public to information from public offices, through streamlining of internal procedures, computerization, and by setting up public facilitation counters in offices by the Government of India and the Governments of the constituent states of the Indian federation. Many of the State Governments of the Indian Federation have enacted the Right to Information Acts and the Union Government has also enacted a Central Right to Information Act in 2005.

One of the other measures adopted in many western countries to ensure transparency in the functioning of the government and to fight corruption and mal-administration is the enactment of Public Interest Disclosure Acts popularly called Whistle-blower Acts. The object of such elements is to improve accountability in government and public sector organizations by encouraging people not to turn a blind eye to mal-practice taking place in their organizations and to report the same to the appropriate authority in a confidential manner or by a public report. Although the Government of India has not been able to enact such an Act, but it has lately been quite concerned to protect the identity and person of such officials, who have dared to come out openly to disclose administrative malpractices to the public. Such a law may soon become a reality as and when the Second ARC's recommendations are implemented.

At the same time in order to provide responsive interface between the citizen and the public services, the Government of India has directed Ministries/Departments and other agencies with public interface to formulate Citizens' Charters, lay down time limits, and standards for services, avenues of citizens' grievances reprisal, and independent scrutiny to ensure implementation of Charters. Simultaneous steps have been taken to introduce "E-Governance" at every level of administration.

Although concerns about the parameters of public ethics in governance have been very well documented in a number of studies both in India and abroad [See for example R.B. Jain, 2000], the Second Administrative Reforms Commission (ARC) in India, under the Chairmanship of Veerappa Moily has made out a very comprehensive study of the issue of ethics in governance in India and has made some significant recommendations in relation to managing ethics in respect of

Legislators, Minister, Civil Servants, Judicial Officers, NGOs, and even on the part of the citizenry at large.

In the realm of public ethics, the Moily Commission has focused on the misuse of office, and has recommended for a new legislation—Corrupt Public Servants (Forfeiture of Property) Bill—so that the State confiscates ill-gotten wealth. It has also recommended for immediate implementation of Benami Transactions (Prohibition) Act. Apart from recommending a legislation to protect Whistle Blowers, by enacting a Whistle Blowers' Act, the second ARC has suggested a new law to tackle serious economic offences involving Rs. 10 crores (approx. 2.2 million USD) and more, and setting of a Serious Frauds Office in Cabinet Secretariat with power to investigate and prosecute in order to discipline financial sector, capital, futures and commodity markets and IT sector. ARC also suggested a law on the lines of American False Commission Act, so that a citizen can seek relief against fraudulent claims against the government. On judiciary, it felt that a National Judicial Commission should lay down the code of conduct of Judges including subordinate judges, recommend names for SC and HC judges, even inquire into cases of misconduct, impose penalties and recommend removal. A Supreme Court Judge should be designated as the Judicial Value Commissioner to enforce the code of conduct. [Second Administrative Reforms Commission, 2007, also see *Times of India,* 13 February 2007, p. 1, Cols. 7, 8, 13, Cols. 1-2 and 1-7].

CONCLUDING OBSERVATIONS

With the tremendous bounce in the economy (more than 8% annual growth in recent years 2009-10), increase in public employment, consumerism, growth of public and private enterprises, basic infrastructure, proliferation of administrative agencies and the enormous burden of public expenditure as a result of the growing socio-economic demands made on the system, the process of administrative development in India has been a continuous one. While the administrative system has at times shown signs of strains due to constant pressures, largely generated by the weight of its own structure and continuous policy changes, the system has certainly acquired some resilience to withstand and bear such pressures. That the public administration in India has not disintegrated, despite a number of dysfunctionalism, pathologies and negative consequences of a growing bureaucratic apparatus lends adequate support to our hypothesis that a complex socio-political structure in a developing society need not always inhibit the processes of administrative development. That does not, however, indicate that public administration in India has been able to hold the highest ethical values in its multifarious activities.

The important requisite for ensuring ethical conduct and probity in governance is absence of corruption, effective laws, rules, and regulations governing every aspect of public life and, more important, an effective and fair implementation of those laws. The NPM movement pointed out to some of ethical concerns borne out of its objectives to reduce the government costs, reduce the number of public employees and change organizational values. While stressing on privatization, the NPM movement does not alter the fact that State has ultimate responsibility as an organizer and has to supervise and control all political and administrative processes, bearing in mind the satisfaction of citizens, and the execution of efficiency, effectiveness, and accountability.

The concept of NPM promotes government transparency, idea of consumer orientation, signifies innovating forms like contracting out, outsourcing of public services, which places a new focus of public ethics on the part of both the civil servants and the new functionaries employed by private and outsourcing agencies for delivery of public services on behalf of the state. Hopefully, the recent adoption of a series of reform measures and devising a number of strategies to bring about transparency and accountability in Indian administration [Jain, 2006, pp. 539-65], viz. : (a) Constitution of Citizen's Charters in Government Departments, (b) Right to Information Act, 2005, (c) Introduction of E-Governance right up to the grass-root levels and the likely implementation of the Second Administrative Reforms Commission's Recommendations on Ethics in Governance (2007) in respect of Proposed Public Service Bill, Whistle Blowing Act, and other steps for promoting ethics among legislators, judicial functionaries and NGOs, may well provide a model for meeting ethical challenges of the impact of globalization and the NPM in governance for possible replication in other countries.

References

Barberis, Peter (1998), The New Public Management and New Accountability. *Public Administration* 76 (Autumn): 451-70.

Bardouille, Nand (2000, January), The Transformation of Governance Paradigms and Modalities. *Round Table No. 353*. 0035-8533: 81-106.

Barzelay, Michael (2001), *The New Public Management: Improving Research and Policy Dialogue*. Berkeley: University of California Press.

Bilhim, Joao, and Barbara Neves "New Ethical Challenges in a Changing Public Administration" (Lisbon, Centre for Public Administration and Policies, University of Lisbon, 2005), Accessed from Googles Network. Pdf Form.

Borins, Sandford (1998), *Innovating With Integrity: How Local Heroes are Transforming American Government*. Washington, D.C.: Georgetown University Press.

Bowornwathana, Bidhya (2001), Politics of Governance Reform in Thailand. In Farazmand, Ali, *Handbook of Comparative and Development Public Administration*. New York: Marcel Dekker, Inc.

Dwivedi. O.P. and R.B. Jain, (1985), *India's Administrative State*, New Delhi, Gitanjali Publishing House.

Ferlie, Ewan, *et. al.* (1996), *The New Public Management in Action*. Oxford; Oxford University Press.

Gore, Al. (1993), *From Red tape to Results: Creating a Government That Works Better & Costs Less: The Report of the National Performance Review.* Washington, D.C. Government Printing Office.

Government of India, Second Administrative Reforms Commission (ARC) (2007), *Report on Ethics in Governance*,. Accessed from *www.gov.arc.nic.in*

Haque, Shamsul M. (1996a). The Contextless Nature of Public Administration in Third World Countries. *International Review of Administrative Sciences.* 62: 315-29.

Harrison, Selig S. (1960), *India : The Most Dangerous Decades*, Princeton; Princeton University Press.

Hood, Christopher. (1991), A Public Management for All Seasons? *Public Administration*. 69(8): 3-19.

Jain, R.B. (2000), "Promoting Ethical Behaviour Amongst Administrators in India", A paper presented at the IPSA Research Committee on SOG Bangalore Conference held on 22-25th March 2000 at Bangalore, Karnataka, India.

———, (2004), *Public Administration in India: 21st Century Challenges for Good Governance* (New Delhi, Deep & Deep Publications (P) Ltd.).

———, (ed.) (2005), *Globalization and Good Governance: Pressures for Constructive Reforms* (New Delhi, Deep & Deep Publications).

Jain, R.B. (2006), "Opening Government for Public Scrutiny: A Critique of Recent Efforts to make Governance in India More Transparent and Accountable" in *Indian Journal of Public Administration,* Vol. 52, No. 3, July-September, pp. 539-65.

———, (ed.) (2007), *Governing Development Across Cultures: Challenges and dilemmas of an emerging sub-discipline in political science* (Opladen, Germany, Barbara Budrich Publishers).

Jain, R.B. and Heinz Bongartz (eds.) (1994), *Structural Adjustment, Public Policy and Bureaucracy in Developing Societies,* New Delhi: Har Anand Publications.

Kashyap, Subhash C. (2006), (ed.) *Constitution of India: Review and Assessment* (Delhi, Universal Law Publishing Co. Pvt. Ltd., 2006), pp. 232-52.

Kim, See Joon-Yang (2005), *A New Paradigm for Public Management in the 21st Century* (Seoul, Korea Institute of Public Administration), pp. 1-32 and 95-152.

Lijphart, Arendt (1996), "The Puzzle of Indian Democracy : A Consociational Interpretation", in *American Political Science Review,* Vol. 90, No. 2 , June.

Mascarenhas, R.C. (1993), Building an Enterprise Culture in the Public Sector: Reform of the Public Sector in Australia, Britain, and New Zealand. *Public Administration Review*. 53(4): 319-28.

Masser, Kai (1998), Public Sector Reforms. In Jay Shafritz, ed., *International Encyclopedia of Public Policy and Administration.* Boulder: Westview Press.

Nolan Report (1995), *Report on Standards in Public Life,* www.archive.official-documents.co.uk/documetns/parliament.

NCRWC, "Summary of the Important Recommendations, 31 March 2002" in Subhash, C. Kashyap (ed.), *Constitution of India: Review and Assessment* (Delhi, Universal Law Publishing Co. Pvt. Ltd., 2006), pp. 232-52.

Osborne, David and Gaebler, T. (1992), *Reinventing Government: How the Entrepreneurial Spirit is Transforming the Public Sector*. Reading: Addison-Wesley.

Reddy, P.L. Sanjeeva (2006), "Improving Delivery Mechanism for Service Excellence" in *Indian Journal of Public Administration,* Vol. 53, No. 3 (July-September), pp. 566-91.

Soni, Vidu (2007), "Public Administration to 'Good Governance' in Developing Countries: The Evolution of a Sub-field in Political Science", in Jain (2007), pp. 84-85.

Times of India, (2007), New Delhi, 13 February 2007, p. 1, Cols. 7, 8, 13, Cols. 1-2 and 1-7.

Conclusion

The Emerging Trends in the Paradigm Shift and Strategies of Development Administration

In the analysis of the evolving concept of development administration that we have made in the foregoing chapters, it can now be discerned that the concept of "Development Administration" is a post-World War II evolution within the discipline of public administration. At the end of World War II, age of imperialism came to an end and the rapid process of de-colonization began. By early 1960s, many of the countries in Africa, Latin America, and Asia, and Middle East, and Asia had gained independence. But along with freedom from colonial rule came the problems of socio-economic development and nation-building. Development had become the dominant issue in these countries, which came to be collectively known as the Third World. The concept of "Development Administration" had become the buzzword not only in the newly emerging societies but also among the Western nations and the UN institutions and documents keen in giving them technical and financial aid to enable them develop.

MEANING OF "DEVELOPMENT ADMINISTRATION"

In simple terms as Edward Weidner has suggested, development administration is synonymous with "an action-oriented, goal-oriented administrative system" (Weidner, 1962: 98). He further defines it as "the process of guiding an organization toward the achievement of developmental objective". Fred Riggs characterized development administration as an administrative problem in government reform. He views development "as a process of increasing autonomy (discretion) of social systems made possible by rising level of diffraction." (Riggs, 1964) Development administration, therefore, encompasses the organization of new agencies such as planning organizations and development corporations, the reorganizations of established agencies such as a department of agriculture, the delegation of administrative powers to development agencies, and the creation of a cadre of administrators who can provide leadership in stimulating and supporting programs of social and economic improvement. It has the purpose of making change attractive and possible. (Gant, 1966: 200-1) Development administration is thus that aspect of public administration that focuses on government induced change towards progressive, political, economic and social objectives.

THE DECADE OF 1960s : THE "INDUCEMENT" PHASE OF DEVELOPMENT ADMINISTRATION

The West responded to the development challenges in a number of ways. Aid and administration for development became mechanisms to fight the war on underdevelopment. It was thought that sufficient foreign aid and a revamped administrative system would allow these former colonies to make similar industrial progress as the West (Dwivedi, 1987). Development goals were usually referred to as nation-building and socio-economic development. Thus, development administration became an essentially "action-oriented, goal-oriented, administrative system geared to realize definite programmatic results". (Dwivedi and Henderson, 1990) The task of developed countries was perceived as the creation of external inducements to change through technical assistance and transfers of technology and institutions. Such strategy of westernization was directed to both the administrative machinery and to the whole national community. A number of techniques such as program planning, community development and personnel management popularized during this era reflect the aforementioned bent for external inducement towards modernization and westernization. A related perception was that institutional imitation was bound to produce similar results to those obtained in the developed world, i.e., efficiency and increased rationality. The more developed an administration system became, the greater the likelihood that it would have developmental effects. (Schaffer, 1973)

THE DECADES OF 70s AND 80s—THE CRISES IN DEVELOPMENT THEORY AND ADMINISTRATION

The early 1970s marked a rude awakening to the inadequacies of the developmental paradigm of public administration to cope with urgent problems. What was peculiar about the crisis of development administration in the seventies was that it became one of identity and purpose with seemingly devastating effects on the entire field of public administration. Assumptions, methodology and focus became increasingly irrelevant. In fact, development administration apparently plunged after the accelerated growth of the sixties into the depth of intellectual depression.

In spite of much rhetoric, the emergent administrative systems tended to be imitative and ritualistic. Generally, practices, styles and structures of administration unrelated to local traditions, needs and realities succeeded in reproducing the symbolism, but not the substance of a western bureaucracy or the administrative system. Over-planning and over-administration tended to have the same negative results (or lack of results) as lack of planning and under-administration. Confronted with an intellectual developmental bureaucracy, the western solution was more administrative development.

Administrative reorganization and rationalization for the sake of abstract principles soon became the ends rather than the means of development administration. The phenomenal expansion of bureaucracy in the Third World countries had a fundamental effect upon the social structure and in many countries bureaucratic authoritarianism has substituted for popular mobilization and mass politics and contradiction between development and social control became sharp. The central issue of development administration then no longer remained just one of manageability of the administrative structure, it became a more fundamental one: the incompatibility between bureaucracy, as a form of institutionalized social control and development—defined as quality of life for the masses.

Thus failures and dysfunctions have been a major source of intrinsic—or internal discontinuity in the dominant thrust of development administration. There have been other or external sources as well, which have been largely the consequences of Third World initiatives and experiences. For many years Western scholars failed to recognize that non-Western contributions to development administration were of any significance. Development administration continued to be a Western concept. The crisis of development administration in the 1980s was thus a consequence of the inability to incorporate the substance of other non-Western development experiences into the emerging conceptual mould.

THE EMERGING FOCUS OF DEVELOPMENT ADMINISTRATION IN 1990s

Whereas the previous development decades emphasized modernization through the transfer of technology (both ideas and tools), assisted by foreign aid, as well as the New International Economic Order, it was acknowledged in the early 1990s that if the coming decade is going to be any relevant for development, it must change its focus and strategy to include such key goals as sustainable development, human resource development, empowerment of specific groups and removal of poverty. Development administration could provide the impetus for the achievement of these core objectives effectively and forcibly. [O.P. Dwivedi, *Development Administration* (New York, St. Martin's Press, 1994, p. 21]

THE IMPACT OF GLOBALIZATION AND STRUCTURAL ADJUSTMENT PROGRAMS : 1990s—THE 'DE-ADMINISTERED DEVELOPMENT'

From the early 1990s onwards the developing countries have been under great pressures emanating out of the forces of globalization, privatization and sustainable development. As a result of the breakdown of the Soviet Union and some of the Eastern European states and the concept of command economy, the emphasis on privatization has led to the reduction in public sector expenditures and personnel. Simultaneously it has led to reduction in role of government, market-friendly economy, de-regulation, divestment, consumerism, and use of business methods in public administration. These issues are being espoused by the World Bank, the IMF and the major donor nations such as the UK, the USA, Canada, Japan, Germany, and the EU. While in the early years, comparative public administration and its protege, development administration were closely associated what was then called "administered development", the new approach is to cut back the scope of government activities through privatisation (particularly of para-statals), deregulation, decentralization and similar efforts, all of which may be subsumed under the rubric 'de-bureaucratization' in other words, a reduction in the scope or at least in the rate of growth, and the streamlining of procedures of the centralized administrative apparatus in the public sector. This was the dominant trend of the 1990s, which led to the changed paradigm of "de-administered development".

THE THRESHOLD OF 21ST CENTURY—THE CONCEPT OF SUSTAINABLE DEVELOPMENT AND THE CORPORATE MILLENNIUM

Ever since the Brundtland Report of 1987, which defined the concept of sustainable development (SD) as "development that meets the needs of the present without compromising the ability of future generations to meet their own needs. . . . A process of change in which exploitation of resources, the direction of investments, the orientation of technology development, and institutional change are all in harmony and e4nhance both current and future potential to meet human needs and aspirations", the central rationale for SD has been to increase people's standaru of living (broadly defined) and, in particular, the well-being of the least advantaged people in societies, avoiding uncompensated future costs. SD highlights the important issue of the sustainability of ecological and social systems rather than economic sustainability alone. SD is also defined as development that improves health care, education and social well-being. Such human development is now recognized as critical to economic development and human prosperity.

The goals of SD can only be achieved by making changes in the present political, economic and technological system at the global level and by making major changes in the management of the planet earth. There is a need to evolve a new global psychology, a fresh way of thinking about political and economic change and society's relationship with nature. International cooperation must develop and continue so that there could be effective global environmental management.

The threshold of the 21st century heralds the advent of the concept of "sustainable development" as also of the "corporate millennium". In the coming years, there is likely to be a growing commitment to a free market and global economy, and therefore corporate governance is going to be a crucial factor in efforts to restructure governing institutions. With the end of the Cold War in the 1980s, the victory of capitalism, the emergence of new industrialized countries around the world and the new technological revolution, political, economic and social phenomena have in many respects bypassed the border of the state and acquired a global dimension. Under globalization, citizen demands are more diversified and sophisticated. They want choice, improved responsiveness and quality of services. With the diminished role of the state, a market-oriented economy supported by a democratic government with an efficient and quality-oriented public administration is conceived as the formula for economic development and well-being of the people. Privatization, deregulation, de-bureaucratization, and decentralization are the current political issues. Performance-oriented governance and management strategies are advocated to improve responsiveness and accountability. No wonder the concept of *development management,* which has gradually expanded to encompass bureaucratic reorientation and restructuring, the integration of politics and culture into management improvement, participatory and performance-based service delivery and program management, community and NGO capacity-building, and policy reform and implementation is increasingly gaining grounds especially in the context of developing countries in place of the earlier emphasis on "administered development" (Brinkerhoff and Coston, 1999, 346-61)

CHANGING PARAMETERS OF DEVELOPMENT ADMINISTRATION

1. The changing parameters and contours of the concept of "Development Administration" have been greatly influenced and affected by the developments in the world environment at every stage of its evolution.
2. Development Administration has not remained merely a sub-field of the discipline of public administration or study in economic growth, but in its evolution has acquired a holistic perspective for an inter-disciplinary approach and study.
3. Foreign aid, Bureaucracy and technological innovations are no longer the only instruments of Development Administration but now also include the various non-state actors and the civil society.
4. Good Governance as an emerging paradigm of Development Administration attempts to provide a more comprehensive framework which reorients the concept of development administration to be more moral, culture specific and the achievements of goals dependent on indigenous efforts.

As the analysis in the foregoing chapters show all these hypotheses stand fully valid. It is important now to analyse the emerging paradigm shift in "development administration"

CONCLUDING OBSERVATIONS : THE EMERGING TRENDS

The Notion of "Good Governance" as a New Paradigm Shift in "Development Administration"

Since the breakdown of the Soviet Union in the 1980s, the discipline of public administration has been tremendously affected by globalization, implementation of the governance model, structural adjustment, market forces, administrative reforms, the New Public Management (NPM) movement, and sharing of knowledge around the world. No wonder, therefore, that at the dawn of the 21st century, Comparative Public Administration (CPA) and Development Administration continue to search for a new focus and a new vision.

The search for a new focus and emphasis has led to a paradigm shift in the concept of Development Administration, which in recent times has been very much dominated by the nuances and requirements of the elusive paradigm of "Good Governance". Increasing global interdependence offers new opportunities for CPA and development administration to revive their earlier premises of institution building. Effective management for good governance is becoming a universal ambition. Thus, modern states are increasingly concerned about the capacities of their institutions and about the need for reorganization so that their institutions can shoulder new responsibilities. The contemporary view of "development" and "development administration" is that there is an overall improvement in productivity and a balanced growth that does not sacrifice environmental concerns or create serious dislocations that disadvantage particular segments of the society (Brinkerhoff and Coston, 1999: 348). Integral to the new development thinking is transparency of public decisions, availability of information, and accountability of public officials and institutions as well as their conscious respect for human rights and values. All these elements form the core of the notion of Good Governance, which marks the latest paradigm shift in the concept of "Development Administration".

Is Governance Reform a Catalyst for Development?

A question has often been raised whether "Governance

Reform" can be a catalyst for development. Many International agencies generally contend that developing countries can boost of economic growth by introducing "good governance" measures. However, an analysis of specific governance reforms and economic turning points in the United States (when it was a developing country), Argentina, Mauritius and Jamaica, carried out recently by Arthur A. Goldsmith of the University of Massachusetts, Boston suggests that the agencies underestimated the time and political effort required to change governance, and overestimate the economic impact. Counter to optimistic claims about how much "institutions matter", these carefully selected cases imply that greater transparency, accountability and participation are often a result, rather than a direct cause of faster development. Furthermore they show that closed institutions may be a satisfactory platform for rapid growth, provided these institutions open over time. Policy-makers need to understand these processes before counting on governance reforms to be the springboard out of poverty for most developing countries today. [Goldsmith, 2007, 165] Given that good governance has many dimensions, governance reform is a dynamic and socially imbedded process and academics and policy-makers should realize that improved civic institutions may not produce perceptibly more efficient governance or many "development dividends" [*Ibid.*, 183].

Shift in Strategies of Development Administration

Thus Governance is a broader concept, which is defined as the exercise of authority through formal and informal traditions and institutions for the common good. "Good Governance" extends beyond the process of selecting, monitoring, and replacing governments. It includes the capacity to formulate and implement sound policies, and it assumes a respect for citizens. From this framework good governance can be construed as consisting of six different elements. These are: (i) voice and accountability, which includes civil liberties and freedom of the press, (ii) political stability, (iii) government effectiveness, which includes the quality of policy-making and public service delivery, (iv) quality of regulations, (v) rule of law, which includes protection of property, rights and an independent judiciary, and (vi) control of corruption. Thus controlling corruption emerges as just one of the most closely intertwined elements of governance. Combating corruption leads to improving governance. The key question therefore is what strategies lower corruption and strengthen good governance? (Kaufman, 2001, 1-3).

Improving governance requires a system of checks and balances in society that restrains arbitrary action and harassment by politicians and bureaucrats, promotes voices and participation by the population, reduces incentives for the corporate elite to engage in state capture, and fosters the rule of law. A meritocratic and service-oriented public administration is a salient feature of such a strategy. However, synthesizing the strategy of key reforms for improving governance and combating corruption is a particularly daunting challenge, as is the task of detailing and adapting a strategy to each country-specific reality. Good Governance is more than fighting corruption. Improving governance should be seen as a process integrating three vital components: (a) knowledge, with rigorous data and empirical analysis, including in-country diagnostics and dissemination, utilizing the latest information technology tools (b) leadership in the political, civil society and international arena; and (c) collective action via systematic participatory and consensus-building approaches with key stake holders in society (for which technology revolution is also assisting). No two countries arrive at the same strategy, but to maximize the prospects of success, any country serious about improving governance must involve all key stakeholders, guarantee a flow of information to them, and lock in the commitment of the leadership *(Ibid.)*.

It may also be noted that in recent times, the bureaucrats, public servants, administrators, policy-makers, implementers and analysts have all acquired tremendous capabilities to face the challenges of development in practical terms through improved methods of training and acquisition of skills not only from the developments in the public sector alone but more often derived from the experiences in the private and business sector. This intermingling and interaction of the professional, technical and specialists' techniques, have given rise to a whole new concept of "administrative sciences", which is now often marketed under the rubric of 'new public management' and 'new management technology'. This has further received tremendous boost with the ongoing revolution in information technology.

Evidently, empirical comparative methodology combined with historical insights and specific case-studies provide great potential for scientific and meaningful understanding of administrative realities in the context of developing societies. And if such studies are conducted on a cross-national basis, this would greatly help in evolving new theories of public bureaucracies, administrative culture and public policies and "good governance". Admittedly, such studies would have to be undertaken with considerable planning, insight, and an adequate knowledge of the unlimited range of variables—more specifically the environmental, political, economic, socio-cultural and the normative variables, that are involved in the play of administrative processes across national frontiers. It may also be desirable to make use of group-efforts in specific research undertakings of this kind in order to critically examine the viability of new paradigms in "development administration".

NEW PARADIGMS OF DEVELOMENT ADMINISTRATION

In its practical concerns, development administration has two aspects; the macro-policy making and the micro-policy implementation which rests on thee basic principles: (a) everything thought or done must be in national or public interest (b) every product the government must benefit the last man of the country and (c) every body should be entitled to know what is happening. Every body talks about governance, but doesn't realize the enormous complexity of working of government. The palpable criticism includes: too many people doing the job and not too efficiently, citizens rightful claims not being realized, conspiracy of politicians and bureaucrats derailing the system. Who is responsible for 63 years of administrative shame? Of course the superior bureaucracy failed to make the government system function. And like Bureaucrats, the political community is also responsible. Together they have destroyed all political institutions. No political party is concerned with reforms, each political leader is interested in short term measures. The continuation of 'Bad Governance' is a crime in which each one of us is a partner. Solutions suggested are only piecemeal and do not tackle the problem completely.

There is no ideal solution to the problems of governance in India, but we must collectively sit down and bring out solutions. The methodology for finding solutions must have 4 cardinal principles : (a) realization that economics and Governance are in highly complicated and complex interplay and relationship; (b) every reform measure must have the art of differential diagnosis; (c) every activity of reform must be accompanied by constant evaluation and monitoring; and (d) external experts must have both personal and institutional commitment to the system.

There are no instant answers to the problems of Good Governance in India. There are example of large number of good reforms, and practices acknowledged and followed, e.g. Cleaning up of Vaishnu Devi Trust in J&K but the pressing need is the reforming of Public Services, which needs three alterantive strategies: (a) to try to develop an honest politico-bureaucratic apparatus that rewards performance and punishes bad work and non-performance; (b) to create a band of dedicated and ethically core of politicians and civil services for implementation of public policies; and (c) to initiate a civil society movement of spreading awareness of rights of people and responsibilities of civil services, demanding performance. The example of the success of recent RWAs efforts in Delhi to oppose hike in electricity tariff, such a movement is in the realm of possibilities. The three areas which need to be reformed are: (a) management of projects; (b) developing appropriate technologies for rural people and rural society; and (c) the strengthening of the provisions and operation of Right to Information Act.

About rural development what the rural population needed was to evolve an efficient cost effective technology to suit to their particular requirements, which could be done through the cooperation of private sector, especially of multi-nationals, which will not utilize the abundant rural manpower which is now a total waste, but would also lead to development of infrastructure, e.g. introduction of Rubber Tyres in Bullock

Carts against the wooden wheels, which added to green revolution during 1960s. The Right to Information Act could be strengthened through creation of increased awareness among the population. The civil society organizations can play a very significant role in this endeavour through net working, pamphlets, guide books, information booklets, etc.

One must also lay stress upon the ethical leadership of the civil services, and the evolution of a Common National Minimum Agenda for public good to be accepted and implemented by all political parties.

There is the need for changing the mindset and psyche of the civil services, if the fruits of the use of IT in governance are to be fully utilized through the cooperation of private sector. It is a shame that amongst the developing countries India has the highest of IT development, but the poorest of its application in governance. One of the main reason is that Indian population is digitally divided. One part of citizens is highly aware and educated, and technologically competent to understand and utilize the digital technology, while the other section, comprising of a majority of citizens is illiterate and technologically ignorant. There is need to bridge this gulf and create a digitally literate population. It is only through electronic governance that transparency, accountability can be obtained in government procedures and the delivery of services to the citizens could be speeded. The concept of electronic kiosks to provide services to citizens at nominal costs may be developed and implemented which will make the E-governance self-sustaining.

India suffers from an absence of governance and most people in India do not have any access to authorities. The question is how much of E governance could enable good governance. A joke prevails around that E-governance means only Election governance. There is a big scope of public-private partnership for providing services to citizens deep down to the rural level. One has to learn lessons from different countries in this respect. It is necessary to have changes in infrastructure and change in attitude of the civil services, which can be done if the concept of CEO of private sector, and its autonomy of functioning with same emoluments and perks is adopted in civil services. Poor infrastructure in government has further hindered the process of decision-making in implementation of projects through E-governance. If properly developed and implemented Government can very fruitfully adopt the techniques of E-governance in three different areas : (a) Police Network, (b Judiciary and legal system, and (c) Delivery of services to citizens.

There is also the requirement to mobilize political and bureaucratic leadership to provide "Technologically Enabled Governance". There is a need to sensitize realm of peoples' awareness through forums of interaction, brainwashing, and networking.

As Professor Ahmed Shafiqul Huque has put it "various theories of development and reactions to them contribute to the process of understanding its enigmatic concept. At the same time they point the need for exploring alternative explanations of the forces and interactions that facilitates such changes. There is obviously a need to identify the aims and objectives that development seeks to achieve. A consensus must be reached on the key elements of the ideal of development and their inter-relationships and interactions discerned. (Huque, 2009, 17)

Modernization of government and public administration involves a redefinition of government responsibilities. The state system of the 21st century, will have to see a redistribution of duties and responsibilities between government, business and society. The guiding principles is the idea of the "empowering state and its people", which leaves more space for society and individual commitment. The internal structures of government administration should also become part of this developmental process. This would require introduction of modern management techniques with quality control, budgeting and cost-benefit analyses. In future, public authorities are meant to be results-oriented in providing public services, Modern management and E-government are two central means of achieving fundamental changes in public administration. The goal is an administration that does more and costs less. In this respect E-government projects are not only modernizing public agencies and authorities, but also making administrative procedures more transparent for ordinary citizens, which in turn also makes new demands on personnel to be more accountable.

Good governance thus included some or all of the following features: an efficient public service; an independent judicial system and legal framework to enforce contracts; the accountable administration of public funds; an independent public auditor, responsible to a representative legislature; respect for the law and human rights at all levels of government; a pluralistic institutional structure, and a free press. The World Bank reconfirmed its initial managerial approach by its 1992 statement in *Governance and Development,* which treats good governance as "synonymous with sound development management". [World Bank, 1992:1] This is the one basic concept, which should be intrinsic to any further evolution of the new paradigms of Development Administration.

References

Brinkrhof, Derek W., Ad Jenifer M. Coston (1999), "International Development Management in a Globalized World" in *Public Administration Review,* July/August 1999, Vol. 59, No. 4, pp. 346-61.

Huque, Ahmed Shafiqul, *The Enigma of Development: Rethinking, Goals, Strategies, Outcomes* (New Delhi, South Asian Publishers, 2009).

Kaufman, Daniel, "New Empirical Frontiers Infighting Corruption and Improving Govenance-Selected Issues", a paper resened at the OSCE Economic Forum (2001), Brusssel, 30-31 January 2001. p. 1.

World Bank, *Governance and Development* (Washington D.C., 2000).

Select Bibliography

A. Primary Sources

Documents

Administration in the 21st Century: Efficient Civil Service and Decentralized Public Administration, Proceedings of the Third International Conference of Administrative Sciences, Brussels.

African Charter (1990).

Cheema, Shabbir (1997). "UNDP Policy and Governance: Conceptual Framework and Development Cooperation."

Speech given at the Good Governance and Democratization Conference in Ottawa on October 16, 1997. http://www.unac.org/events/goodgov/part1.html

Current Research in Social Sciences in Universities and Colleges/by Indian Council of Social Science Research, .New Delhi: Indian Council of Social Science Research, 1971.

International Institute of Administrative Sciences (1995). *Administration and Society.*

Administrative Response to Globalization and Socio-Cultural change, Proceedings of XIII Congress of Administrative Sciences, Brussels.

International Institute of Administrative Sciences (1997). *New Challenges for Public Administration.*

Ivan Doherty (2001). "Democracy Out of Balance—Civil Society can't Replace Political Parties." *Policy Review*, April/May *(http://www.ndi.org/globalp/polparties/polparties.asp*

OECD (1995). *Governance in Transition: Public Management Reforms in OECD Countries.* OECD: Paris.

OECD Development Assistance Committee. (1996). *Shaping the 21st Century: The Contribution of Development Assistance.* Paris: OECD.

UNDP. (1993). *Report on Public Administration Sector Study.* United Nations Development Program.

United Nations. (1983). *Enhancing Capabilities for Administrative Reform in Developing Countries.* Department of Technical Cooperation. New York.

United Nations Program in Public Administration and Finance. (2000). *Managerial Response to Globalization.* Draft Report. Fifteenth Session, May 8-12.

World Bank, Global Economic Prospects: Realizing the Development Promise of the Doha Agenda, Washington, DC, World Bank, 2003. 2 Vols.

World Bank (1992), Governance *and Development* (Washington DC, World Bank.

World Bank (1994), *World Development Report, 1994: Infrastructure for Development.* New York: Oxford University Press.

World Bank (1994). *The World Development Report.* Washington, DC, The World Bank.

World Bank Website: *http://info.worldbank.org/governance/kkz2002/index.htm*

World Commission on Environment and Development (1987), *Our Common Future, A Report.*

B. Secondary Sources

Books and Periodical Literature

Aberbach, Joel D. and Rockman, Bert A. (1988). Problems of Cross-National Comparison. In D.C. Rowat. Ed. *Public Administration in Developed Democracies.* New York: Marcel Dekker.

Almond, Gabriel, A. *et. al.* (2000). *Comparative Politics Today: A World View,* New York: Longman.

Asmerom, H.K., Hoppe, R. and Jain, R.B., Eds. (1992). *Bureaucracy and Development*al Policies *in the Third World*. Amsterdam: University Press.

Asmerom, H.K. and Jain, R.B., Ed. (1993). *Politics, Administration and Public Policy in Developing Countries*. Amsterdam: VU University Press.

Aucoin, Peter (1990). Administrative Reform in Public Management: Paradigms, Principles, Paradoxes and Pendulums. *Governance: An International Journal of Policy and Administration*. 3(2): 115-37.

Ayee, Joseph R. (1998). *Africa in Chaos*. New York: St. Martins Press.

Baker, Randall, Ed. (1994). *Comparative Public Management: Putting U.S. Public Policy and Implementation in Context*. Westport: Praeger.

Baker, R. (1991). The Role of State and Bureaucracy in Developing Countries Since World War II. In Ali Farazmand (ed.) *Handbook of Comparative and Development Administration*. New York: Marcel Dekker, Inc.

Balogun, M.J. (2002). The Democratization and Development Agenda and the African Civil Service: Issues Resolved or Matters Arising? *International Review of Administrative Sciences*. 68(4): 533-56.

Barberis, Peter. (1998). The New Public Management and New Accountability. *Public Administration* 76 (Autumn): 451-70.

Bardouille, Nand (2000, January). The Transformation of Governance Paradigms and Modalities. *Round Table No. 353*. 0035-8533: 81-106.

Barzelay, Michael (2001). *The New Public Management*: Improving Research and Policy Dialogue. Berkeley: University of California Press.

Bhattacharya, Mohit (1998). Conceptualizing Good Governance. *Indian Journal of Public Administration*. 54(3): 289-96.

Blunt, Peter. 1995. "Cultural Relativism, Good Governance and Sustainable Human Development," *Public Administration and Development*, 15.

Borins, Sandford (1998). *Innovating With Integrity: How Local Heroes are transforming American Government*. Washington, DC, Georgetown University Press.

Bowornwathana, Bidhya (2001). Politics of governance Reform in Thailand. In Farazmand, Ali. *Handbook of Comparative and Development Administration,* New York, Marcel Dekker, Inc.

Braibanti, Ralph. (1966). Transnational Inducement of Administrative Reform: A Survey of Scope and Critiques of Issues. In J.D. Montgomery and W.J. Siffin (Eds.) *Approaches to Development: Politics, Administration and Change*. New York: McGraw Hill.

Brinkerhoff, Derick, and Coston, Jennifer (1999). International Development Management in a Globalized World. *Public Administration Review*. 59 (4): 346-61.

Buerkle, Tom and Friedman. (2001). Globalization Foes Have Their Say. *International Herald Tribune*. (January 27).

Caiden, Gerald E. (1994). Administrative Reforms. In Randall Baker, Ed. (1994). *Comparative Public Management: Putting U.S. Public Policy and Implementation in Context.* Westport: Praeger.

Caiden, Gerald and Caiden, Naomi (1990). Towards the Future of Comparative Public Administration. In Dwivedi, O.P. and Henderson, Keith M., Eds. (1990). *Public Administration in World Perspective.* Ames: Iowa State University Press.

Caiden, Gerald E. (1994). Globalizing the Theory and Practice of Public Administration. In Garcia-Zamor, Jean-Claude and Khotor, Renu., Eds. *Public Administration in the Global Village.* Westport: Praeger Publishers.

Caiden, Gerald E. (2001). Administrative Reform. In Farazmand, (Ed.) *Handbook of Comparative and Development Public Administration.* New York: Marcel Dekker, Inc.

Caldwell, Lynton K. (1965). Conjectures On Comparative Public Administration. In Roscoe Martin, Ed. *Public Administration and Democracy: Essays in Honor of Paul H. Appleby.* New York, Syracuse University Press.

Carneiro, J.P. (1982). *National Debureaucratization Program: Three Years of Debureaucratization.* National Debrueacratization Program, Brasilia.

Chandler, J.A. ed. (2000). *Comparative Public Administration, London, Routledge.*

Chaturvedi, T.N. Ed. (1985). Administrative Reform-Revisited. *Indian Journal of Public Administration.* 31(3).

Chaudhry, Shahid A. (1994). Role of the World Bank in Civil Service Reform. In Chaudhry *et al.*, Eds. *Civil Service Reform in Latin America and the Caribbean.* Washington, DC, World Bank Technical Paper Number 259.

Chaudhry, Amjad; Reid, Gary J; and Malik, Waleed, H.; Eds. (1994). *Civil Service Reform in Latin America and the Caribbean.* Washington, D.C. World Bank Technical Paper Number 259.

Cheung, A.B. (1997). Understanding Public Sector Reforms: Global Trends and Diverse Agendas. *International Review of Administrative Sciences.* 63: 435-457.

Conyers, D. (1983). Decentralization: The Latest fashion in Development Administration. *Public Administration and Development.* 3(2): 97-109.

Cooper, Phillip J. *et al.*, Eds. (1998). *Public Administration for the Twenty-First Century.* Orlando: Harcourt Brace College Publishers.

Das, S.K. (1998). *Civil Service Reform and Structural Adjustment.* Oxford: Oxford university Press.

Deme (1997). The Problems of Privatization: The Experience of Sub-Saharan African Countries. *International Review of Administrative Sciences.* 63: 79-97.

Dibie, Robert and Herron, Sharron, Y. (2002). Nigerian Public Administrators: Perception of the Importance of Managerial Skills. *International Journal of Public Administration.* 25 (8): 931-51.

Dwivedi, O.P. and Henderson, Keith M. (1990). State of the Art: Comparative Public Administration and Development Administration. In Dwivedi, O.P. and Henderson, Keith M., Eds. (1990). *Public Administration in World Perspective.* Ames: Iowa State University Press.

Dwivedi, O.P. and Nef, J. (1982). Crises and Continuities in Development Theory and Administration. *Public Administration and Development.* 2(1): 59-77.

Dwivedi, O.P. Ed. (1987). *Perspectives on Technology and Development.* New Delhi, Gitanjali.

Dwivedi, O.P. and R.B. Jain (1985). *India's Administrative State.* New Delhi, India: Gitanjali Publishing House.

Dwivedi, O.P. (1987). Moral Dimensions of Statecraft: A Plea for n Administrative Theology", *Canadian Journal of Political Science,* Vol. 20, No. 4, December, pp. 699-709.

———, Ed. (1987). *Perspectives on Technology and Development.* New Delhi: Gitanjali.

———, Eds. (1990). *Public Administration in World Perspective.* Ames: Iowa State University Press.

Dwivedi, O.P. (1994), *Development Administration: From Underdevelopment to Sustainable Development* (New York, St. Martin's Press).

———, (1995). "Reflections on Moral Government and Public Service as a Vocation", *Indian Journal of Public Administration,* Vol. 41, No. 3, July-September, pp. 296-306.

Dwivedi, O.P. and James Ian Gow (1999). *From Bureaucracy to Public Management: The Administrative Culture of the Federal Government of Canada.* Peterborough, Canada, Broadview Press.

Dwivedi, O.P. (2002). "On Common Good and Good Governance: An Alternative Approach" in *Better Governance and Public Policy: Capacity Building and Democratic Renewal in Africa.* Edited by Dele Olowu and Soumana Sako. Bloomfield, CT, USA: Kumarian Press, pp. 35-51.

———, (2002), "The Challenge of Cultural Diversity for Good Governance", *The Indian Journal of Public Administration,* 48, pp. 14-28.

———, (2002). Challenges in Public Administration in Developing Nations. *In the Turning World: Globalization and Governance at the Start of the 21st Century,* ed. G. Bertucci and M. Duggett, 47-54. Amsterdam: IOS Press.

———, (2003). "In the matter of Good Governance: A Non-western Perspective", Draft of the Revised paper, earlier presented at the World Congress of Political Science held in Quebec City, Canada in 2000. Revised 30.4.2003.

Esman, Milton (1991). *Management Dimensions of Development: Perspectives and Strategies*. West Hartford: Kumarian Press.

———, (1966). The Politics of Development Administration. In John D. Montgomery and William J. Siffin. Ed. *Approaches to Development: Politics, Administration, and Change*. New York: McGraw Hill.

Farazmand, Ali (1999a). Privatization or Reform? Public Enterprise Management in Transition. *International Review of Administrative Sciences*. 65(4): 551-67

———, (1999b). Globalization and Public Administration. *Public Administration Review*. 59(6): 509-22.

———, (2001a). Comparative and Development Public Administration: Past, Present, and Future. In Farazmand, (Ed.) *Handbook of Comparative and Development Public Administration*. New York: Marcel Dekker, Inc.

———, (2001b). *Handbook of Comparative and Development Public Administration*. New York: Marcel Dekker, Inc.

———, (1994). Bureaucracy, Bureaucratization, and De bureaucratization in Ancient and Modern Iran. In A. Farazmand, Ed. *Handbook of Bureaucracy*. New York: Marcel Dekker.

———, (ed.) (2009). Bureaucracy and Administration (Boca Raton, Fl., 2009).

Feldman, Elliot. (1978). Comparative Public Policy: Field or Method. *Comparative Politics*. (January): 287-303.

Ferlie, Ewan, *et al.* (1996). *The New Public Management in Action*. Oxford; Oxford University Press.

Gant, G.F. (1979). *Development Administration: Concepts, Goals, Methods*. Madison: University of Wisconsin Press.

Garcia-Zamor, Jean-Claude and Khator, Renu. (1994). *Public Administration in the Global Village*. Wesport: Preager Publishers.

Garcia-Zamor, Jean-Claude (2001). Problems of Public Policy Implementation in Developing Countries. In Farazmand, Ali. *Handbook of Comparative and Development Public Administration*. New York: Marcel Dekker, Inc.

Goldsmith, Arthur A. (1999). Africa's Overgrown State Reconsidered: Bureaucracy and Economic Growth. *World Politics*. 51(4): 520-46.

Goldsmith, Arthur A. (2007), "Is Governance Reform a Catalyst for Development?" in *Governance,* Vol. 26, No. 2 (April 2007), 165-86.

Gore, Al (1993). *From Red Tape to Results: Creating a Government That Works Better & Costs Less: The Report of the National Performance Review.* Washington, DC, Government Printing Office.

Gould, David J. (2001). Administrative Corruption: Incidence, Causes, and Remedial Strategies. In Farazmand (Ed.), *Handbook of Comparative and Development Public Administration.* New York: Marcel Dekker, Inc.

Gould, David J. and Amaro-Reyes, J.A. (1983). *The Effects of Corruption on Administrative Performance: Illustrations from Developing Countries.* World Bank. Washington, DC.

Graham, L.S. (1980). Centralization versus Decentralization in the Administration of Public Service. *International Review of Administrative Sciences.* 46 (3): 219-32.

Greenway, J.R. (1984). Bureaucrats Under Pressure: The Thatcher Government and the Mandarin Elite. *Teaching Politics.* 13(1): 66-84.

Hammergren, L.A. (1983). *Development and Politics of Administrative Reform: Lessons from Latin America.* Boulder: Westview Press.

Haque, Shamsul M. (1996a). The Contextless Nature of Public Administration in Third World Countries. *International Review of Administrative Sciences.* 62: 315-29.

———, (1996b). Public Service Under Challenge in the Age of Privatization. *Governance.* 9(2): 186-216.

———, (1994). The Emerging Challenges to Bureaucratic Accountability: A Critical Perspective. In Ali Farazmand (ed.). *Handbook of Bureaucracy.* New York: Marcele Dekker.

Harrison, Neil E. (1998). Why Science and Technology Require Political Guidance to Sustain Development. *Politics and the Life Sciences.* 17(2): 179-88.

Haruna, Peter F. (2003). Reforming Ghana's Public Service: Issues and Experiences in Comparative Experiences in Comparative Perspectives. *Public Administration Review.* 63(3):329-42.

Heady, Ferrel (2001). *Public Administration: A Comparative Perspective.* (6th edition). New York: Marcel Dekker, Inc.

———, (1990). Introduction. In Dwivedi, O.P. and Henderson, Keith M., Eds. *Public Administration in World Perspective.* Ames: Iowa State University Press.

Heady Ferrel, and Stokes, Sybil L. (1962). *Papers in Comparative Public Administration.* Ann Arbor: Institute of Public Administration.

Heady, Ferrel (1998). Comparative and International Public Administration: Building Intellectual Bridges. *Public Administration Review.* 58(1):32-39.

———, (1978). Comparative Administration: A Sojourner's Outlook. *Public Administration Review.* 38(4):358-65.

Henderson, Keith M. (1971). A New Comparative Public Administration. In Frank Marini (Ed.) *Towards a New Public administration*. Scranton: Chandler Publishing.

———, (1990). Rethinking the Comparative Experience: Indigenization *versus* Internationalization. In Dwivedi, O.P. and Henderson, Keith M., Eds. *Public Administration in World Perspective.* Ames: Iowa State University Press.

———, (1995). Reinventing Comparative Public Administration: Indigenization Models of Study and Application. *International Journal of Public Sector Management.* 8(4): 17-25.

———, (1971). A New Comparative Public Administration. In Frank Marini. Ed. *Towards a New Public Administration.* Scranton: Chandler Publishing.

Hofstede, Geert. (1984). Cultural Dimensions in Management and Planning. *Asia Journal of Management.* (January): 81-99.

Hood, Christopher. (1991). A Public Management for All Seasons? *Public Administration.* 69(8): 3-19.

Hummel, Ralph P. (1994). *The Bureaucratic Experience.* New York: St. Martin's Press.

Huque, Ahmed Shafiqul and Habib Zafarullah (2006), *International Development Governance* (Boca Raton, Taylor and Francis, 2006).

Huque, Ahmed Shafiqul, (2009), *The Enigma of Development: Rethinking, Goals, Strategies, Outcomes* (New Delhi, South Asian Pblishers, 2009).

International Institute of Administrative Sciences .(1997). *New Challenges for Public Administration.*

Ivan Doherty (2001). "Democracy out of Balance—Civil Society can't Replace Political Parties." *Policy Review*, April/May *(http://www.ndi.org/globalp/polparties/polparties.asp*

Izquierdo, Alejandro, "Sudden Stops, the Real Exchange Rate and Fiscal Sustainability in Argentina," *The World Economy.* Volume 25, No. 7, July 2002, pp. 903-23.

Jabbra, Joseph G. and O.P. Dwivedi, eds. (1987). *Public Service Accountability: Comparative Perspectives.* West Hartford, Conn. USA, Kumarian Press.

Jain, R.B. (2001). Toward Good Governance: A Half Century of India's Administrative Development. *International Journal of Public Administration.* 24(12): 1299-1334.

———, (2000). Bureaucracy and Development in the Third World: Emerging Trends in Good Governance at the Threshold of Twenty First Century. Unpublished Conference Paper. *XVIII World Congress of the International Political Science Association.*

———, (1971), "Research Methods in Public Administration: A critical Study of Important Works in Historical and Comparative Methodology", *Indian Journal of Public Administration*, Vol. XVII, No. 4, October-December 1971.

———, (1976). *Contemporary Issues in Indian Administration*, Vishal Publications, Delhi, India.

———, (1978), "Comparative Aspects of Public Administration", in Robin W. Winks (ed.), *Other Voices, Other Views*, Westport, Greenwood Press, 1978, pp. 260 ff.

Jain, R.B. and P.N. Chaudhury (1984), *Bureaucratic Values in Development* (New Delhi, Centre for Policy Research, Uppal Publishing House.), Especially see the Chapter on Review of Literature, pp. 1-31.

Jain, R.B. (ed.), (1989), *Bureaucratic Politics in the Third World* (New Delhi, Gitanjali Publishing House, 1989.

———, (ed.), (1995), *NGOs in Development Perspective* (Delhi, Vivek Prakashan, 1995).

Jain, R.B. (2000). Bureaucracy and Development in the Third World: Emerging Trends in Good Governance at the Threshold of Twenty-first Century. Unpublished Conference Paper. *XVIII World Congress of the International Political Science Association.*

———, (2002). *Public Administration in India: 21st Century Challenges for Good Governance.* New Delhi, Deep & Deep Publications.

———, (2001). Toward Good Governance: A Half Century of India's Administrative Development. *International Journal of Public Administration.* 24(12): 1299-1334.

———, (2004) *Corruption-free Sustainable Development: Challenges and Strategies for Good Governance.* (New Delhi: Mittal Publications)

———, (2004), "Good Governance for Sustainable Development: Challenges and Strategies in India, *The Indian Journal of Public Administration,* Vol. 50, January March. Special Issue on Governance.

———, (2005), *Globalization and Good Governance: Pressure for Constructive Reforms* (New Delhi, Deep & Deep Publications (P) Ltd., 2005.

———, (2009), "Socio-political Structure and Public Administration in India" in Farazmand (2009), pp. 495-528.

———, (2006), Good Governance, Bureaucracy, and Development: Have the Traditioal Bureaucratic Values become Redundant? In Huque and Zafarullah (2006), pp. 529-44.

———, (2007), *Governing Development Across Cultures* (Germany, Budrich and Budrich Publishers.

Jreisat, Jamil E. (2002). *Comparative Public Administration and Policy.* Colorado: Westview Press.

———, (1999). Comparative Public Administration and Reform. *International Journal of Public Administration.* 22(6):855-77.

———, (2001). The Organizational Perspective in Comparative and Development Administration. In Farazmand, Ali. *Handbook of Comparative and Development Public Administration.* New York: Marcel Dekker, Inc.

Jun, John (1976). Reviewing the Study of Comparative Administration: Some Reflections on the Current Possibilities. *Public Administration Review*. 36(6): 645.

Kettl, Donald (1997). The Global Revolution in Public Management: Driving Themes and Missing Links. *Journal of Policy Analysis and Management*. 16(3):446-62.

———, (2001). The Transformation of Governance: Globalization, Devolution, and the Role of Government. *Public Administration Review*. 60(6):488-97.

———, (2000). *The Global Public Management Revolution*. Washington, DC, Brookings Institution.

———, (1993). *Sharing Power: Governance and Private Markets*. Washington, DC, Brookings Institution.

Khan, M.M. (1980a). Ruling Elites and Major Administrative Reforms: The Case of Pakistan Civil Service. *Indian Journal of Political Science*. 24(2): 170-80.

———, (1980b). Administrative Reform. *Indian Journal of Public Administration*. 24(2): 170-80.

Khator, Renu (1998). The New Paradigm : From Development Administration to Sustainable Development Administration. *International Journal of Public Administration*. 21(12): 1777-1802.

Korten, D. (1990). *When Corporations Rule the World*. West Hartford: Kumarian Press.

Lan, Z. and Rosenbloom, D. (1992). Editorial. *Public Administration Review*. 52(6): 535-37.

Lane, Frederic S. (1999) *Current Issues in Public Administration*. Boston: Bedford/St. Martin's.

Leftwich, Adrian (1994). Governance, the State and the Politics of Development. *Development and Change*. 25: 363-86.

Lynn, Laurence E. (1998). The New Public Management: How to Transform a Theme Into a Legacy. *Public Administration Review*. 58(3): 231-37.

Mascarenhas, R.C. (1993). Building an Enterprise Culture in the Public Sector: Reform of the Public Sector in Australia, Britain, and New Zealand. *Public Administration Review*. 53(4):319-328.

Masser, Kai (1998). Public Sector Reforms. In Jay Shafritz, ed., *International Encyclopedia of Public Policy and Administration*. Boulder: Westview Press.

Mathur, Kuldeep (1986). Whither Public Administration? In Kuldeep Mathur (ed.) *A Survey of Research in Public Administration* (New Delhi, Concept).

Minocha, O.P. (1997). Good Governance: Concept and Operational Issues. *Management in Government*. (October-December).

Montgomery, John D. (1991). The Strategic Environment of Public Managers in Developing Countries. In Farazmand, Ali. *Handbook of Comparative and Development Public Administration*. New York: Marcel Dekker, Inc.

Naim, Moises (1994). Public Bureaucracies in Developing Countries: Ten Paradoxes. In Chaudhry, Amjad; Reid, Gary J. and Malik, Waleed, H.; Eds. *Civil Service Reform in Latin America and the Caribbean*. Washington, DC, World Bank Technical Paper Number 259.

Sborne, David and Gaebler, T. (1992). *Reinventing Government: How the Entrepreneurial Spirit is Transforming the Public Sector*. Reading: Addison-Wesley.

Peters, Guy B. (1994). New Visions of Government and the Public Service. In Patricia W. Ingrahm and Barbra S. Romzek, eds., *New Paradigms for Government: Issues for Changing Public Service*. San Francisco: Jossey Bass.

Pollitt, Christopher. (1990). *Managerialism and the Public Services: The Anglo-American Experience*. Oxford: Blackwell.

Qua, Jon, S.T. (1982). Bureaucratic Corruption, in the Asian Countries: A Comparative Analysis of their Anti-Corruption Strategies. *Journal of Southeast Asian Studies*. (13(1).

Riggs, Fred W. (1998). Public Administration: A Futuristic Vision. *International Journal of Public Administration Review*, 21(12): 1667-1758.

———, (1994). Global Forces and the Discipline of Public Administration. In Garcia-Zamor, Jean-Claude and Khotor, Renu, Eds. *Public Administration in the Global Village*. Wesport: Preager Publishers.

———, (1991). Public Administration: A Comparativist Framework. *Public Administration Review.*, 51(6): 473-84.

———, (1964). *Administration in Developing Countries: The Theory of Prismatic Society*. Boston: Houghton Mifflin.

Riggs, Fred (1961). *The Ecology of Public Administration.* New Delhi: Asia Publishing House.

Rosenbloom, David H. and Kravchuk, Robert S. (2002). *Public Administration: Understanding Management, Politics, and Law in the Public Sector.* New York: McGraw Hill.

Rowan, Miranda and Lerner, Allan (1995). Bureaucracy, Organizational Redundancy, and the Privatization of Public Sector. *Public Administration Review.* 55(2):193-200.

Ryan, Richard (1994). The Importance of Comparative Study in Educating the U.S. Public Service. In R. Baker (Ed.) Westport: Praeger.

Savas, E.S. (1987). *Privatization: The Key to Better Government.* Chatham: Chatham House.

Schaffer, Bernard (1973). *The Administrative Factor.* London: Frank Cass.

Shihata, Ibrahim, F. (1994). Administrative Reform in Developing Countries: Some General Observations. In Chaudhry, Amjad; Reid, Gary J.; and Malik, Waleed, H., Eds. *Civil Service Reform in Latin America and the Caribbean.* Washington, DC, World Bank Technical Paper Number 259.

Siffin, William J. (1991). The Problem of Development Administration In Farazmand, Ali. *Handbook of Comparative and Development Public Administration.* New York: Marcel Dekker, Inc.

Siffin, W.J. Ed. (1957). *Towards the Comparative Study of Public Administration.* Bloomington: Indiana University Press.

Soni, Vidu (2003). "Public Administration and Governance in Developing Countries in the Last Quarter Century: A Status Report, A paper prepared for IPSA Political Science Development 2000 Project, 2003, p. 6.

Subramaniam, V., Ed. (1990). *Public Administration in the Third World.* Westport: Greenwood Press, Inc.

Thakoor, Persaud and Malik, Waleed H. (1994). The Impact of Socio-cultural and Governance Factors on Institutional Reform. In Chaudhry *et al.* Eds. *Civil Service Reforms in Latin America and the Caribbean.* Washington, DC, World Bank Technical Paper Number 259.

The Economist (2000). No Gain Without Pain: Why the Transition to E-Government will Hurt, *The Economics Ltd.* (June 24): 9-14.

Thomas, Vinod (1999). Globalization: Implications for Development Learning. *Public Administration and Development.* 19 (1): 5-17.

Tummala, K.K. (1979). *The Ambiguity of Ideology and Administrative Reform.* Bombay: Allied Publishers.

Vigoda, Eran (2002). From Responsiveness to Collaboration: Governance, Citizens, and the Next Generation of Public Administration. *Public Administration Review.* 62(5):527-540.

Waldo, Dwight. (1980). *The Enterprise of Public Administration.* Novato: Chandler and Sharp.

Waldo, Dwight (1964). *Comparative Public Administration: Prologue, Problems, and Promise.* Chicago: American Society for Public Administration.

Weber, Max (1958). *From Max Weber: Essays in Sociology.* In H.H. Gerth and C.W. Mills, trans. and eds. New York: Oxford University Press.

Welch, Eric and Wong, Wilson (1998). Public Administration in a Global Context: Bridging the Gaps of Theory and Practice between Western and Non-Western Nations. *Public Administration Review.* 58(1):40-49.

Werlin, Herbert H. (2003). Poor Nations, Rich Nations: A Theory of Governance. *Public Administration Review.* 63(3):329-42.

Williams, R. (1987). *Political Corruption in Africa.* Gower: Aldershot.

Wilson, Woodrow (1887). The Study of Administration. *Political Science Quarterly.* 56 (December 1941): 494.

World Bank (1992). *Governance and Development.* Washington, DC.

World Bank (1994). *World Development Report, 1994: Infrastructure for Development.* New York: Oxford University Press.

Zafarullah, Habib and Huque, Ahmed S. (2001). Public Management for Good Governance: Reforms, Regimes, and Reality in Bangladesh. *International Journal of Public Administration.* 24(12): 1379-1403.

Index